Modern Japanese Poetry

translated by
JAMES KIRKUP

edited and introduced by
A.R. DAVIS

University of Queensland Press

© University of Queensland Press, St. Lucia, Queensland
1978

Printed and bound by Silex Enterprise & Printing Co.,
Hong Kong

Distributed in the United Kingdom, Europe, the Middle
East, Africa, and the Caribbean by Prentice-Hall Internat-
ional, International Book Distributors Ltd., 66 Wood Lane
End, Hemel Hempstead, Herts., England

Published with the assistance of the Literature Board of the
Australia Council

National Library of Australia
Cataloguing-in-Publication data
Modern Japanese poetry.

(Asian and Pacific writing).
ISBN 0 7022 1148 6.

1. Japanese poetry. I. Kirkup, James Falconer,
1918–, tr. II. Davis, Albert Richard, ed. (Series)

895.6'08

In grateful and affectionate memory of

MURANO SHIRŌ (1901–75)

Acknowledgments

Some of these translations first appeared in *Japan Quarterly*: *Poetry Australia*; *Modern Poetry in Translation*; *London Magazine*; *Orient–West*; *Prism International*; *Poetry Nippon*; *Mundus Artium*; *Times Literary Supplement*; *Eigo Kyōiku* (Tokyo); *Poetry and Audience* (Leeds University); *Loon*, (USA) and *Japanese Writing Today* (Penguin).

Satō Haruo's "The Song of the Mackerel Pike" appeared in *Shepherding Winds*, edited by James Kirkup (Blackie).

Takagi Kyōzō's "The Winter Moon" and "Sick Submarine" appeared in *Selected Poems of Takagi Kyozo*, introduced and translated by James Kirkup and Nakano Michio (Carcanet Press).

Contents

*References in brackets are to *Nihon Shijin Zenshū* in thirty-
four volumes published by Shinchōsha, Tokyo, 1967–69.
When a translation is not given of the title of a poet's
collection, it will be found in the Biographical Notes.

xiii   CONTENTS

xxv   CONTENTS

Introduction
by General Editors

Asian and Pacific Writing is a series making accessible to English readers some of the world's most exciting and dynamic new literatures. The primary concern is with modern and contemporary work. The series contains both translations and work written originally in English, both volumes by single writers and anthologies. The format is flexible so that it can respond to the variety of an area that spans the world's oldest and youngest literary traditions. A forum for contemporary writers and translators in Asia and the Pacific, the series gives expression to an expanding literature outside of the European, Soviet, and American cultural blocs. Edited and published from Australia, Asian and Pacific Writing marks Australia's developing awareness of her place in Asia. And it marks, too, an international mood of literary exploration, an interest in new forms and new stimuli, a spreading interest in getting to know other cultures, a determination to break down language and other barriers that have prevented literary interchange.

Michael Wilding

Harry Aveling

Translator's Preface
by James Kirkup

"Poetry", said Robert Frost, "is what is lost in translation." A rather glib statement by a poet who was not a translator himself. However, it must be admitted that in most translations of poetry, it is the poetry that vanishes, leaving only heaps of dead words. But it need not always be so.

It takes a poet to translate a poet. Or at least a translator with the mind and imagination of a poet. Such translators are very rare. What the translators do is transfer the words of one language into the words of another, more or less accurately. What the poets do is pour carefully the wine of a poem from the bottle of one language into the decanter of another. It is the soul of the wine that concerns them most, and no matter if there are a few splashes and overflows. The poets find the roots of the poem's spirit in its words, its form, its imagery, its poetic devices, its punctuation or lack of it, its shape upon the page. For them, a translated poem must not be just a translation, but a living, breathing work of art in its own right.

It is always as a poet that I have tried to approach the translation of poetry. In the poet being translated I try to find my alter ego, try to get into his skin and bones, to feel him breathing, to get into the rhythm of his thought, to identify myself with him completely, without losing anything of my own poetic being. Of this passionate marriage poetic translations are born. I listen for that individual way of speaking that always indicates a true poet. I listen to his pauses, hesitations, and silences, attend to the gaps between the words and between the lines. I observe his unique choice of words, ordinary words which he makes somehow into something rich and strange. I get the music first, and the beat, and the meaning follows after.

This is how I have always worked in my translations of

European poetry. With European poets I have a common European background. It is easy to identify with them. But can a Westerner identify himself completely with an Oriental, when their social, cultural, and geographical backgrounds are so dissimilar?

I have been fortunate to live in Japan and other Far Eastern and South-East Asian countries for many years. As I said in my first book about Japan, *These Horned Islands*, I felt immediately at home as soon as I set foot on the shores of Japan. At once I had the unmistakable feeling that I had lived there in a previous existence—sure proof to me of reincarnation. Even before I learnt any Japanese—and for years I resisted learning the language, preferring the language of silence which only Orientals instinctively understand—I was able to enter into the true heart of Japan as I believe no other Westerner has ever done. After all, Westerners and Orientals are all human beings: there is no need for us to be strangers to one another. Like the infamous "language barrier", there is no human barrier if one does not erect one.

Poetry is so much more than words. Every poem is an essence, a distillation of a whole lifetime, a whole civilization, through a vision or an insight which may have lasted only a microsecond but which is eternalized in a breath, a sigh, a shout of joy or indignation, a laugh, a song, a prayer, an expression of impossible longing.

Contemporary Japanese poetry is all these things. It represents essences of human experience, often in grotesque surrealist imagery, but also in styles and attitudes which are only Japanese. But in order to understand the poetry properly one must have lived in Japan, experienced all the curious varieties of life and refinements of culture there. One must have entered into the bodies and souls of Japanese people, observing the way they think and move and behave, and listened patiently to their telling silences, which are so much a part of their poetry. My intimate familiarity with the ordinary life of Japan helped me more than anything else to understand the roots of these poems and to make the roots bear branches, leaves, flowers, and fruit in English.

From a practical point of view, I pursued several methods, together or separately. As I do not read Japanese well enough, I had some of the poems transcribed into *romaji*, which, with the aid of dictionaries, I was able to read. Of course the important visual beauty of the language, with its tremulous reverberations of meaning and its haunting ambiguities, are largely lost by this method. However, I was able to have certain ancient and complex *kanji* or ideographs explained to me with all their richness of association.

Many of the poems were read to me aloud, though to an English poet accustomed to the lyrical and rhythmical reading-aloud of poetry, Japanese poets sound flat and inexpressive. Contemporary Japanese poetry is very close to the rhythms and vocabulary of daily speech, incorporating slang and foreign words, so it was illuminating and useful to listen to the poems being read aloud.

Another method, one I most enjoyed, was to work in close collaboration with the poet himself, and here I have been especially privileged to have the advice and insights of the late Murano Shirō, of Takahashi Mutsuo, Shibuya Haruo (who also helped me with some of Murano's poems), Takagi Kyōzō, Kihara Kōichi, Tanikawa Shuntarō, and Nishiwaki Junzaburō, my colleague at Japan Women's University. Takagi Kyōzō and Takahashi Mutsuo were so kind as to send me their very latest work, and Mr Takahashi himself selected his four favourite poems for me—the four "Portraits" from *Watakushi*.

In a kind of reverse process, I was able to help the growing number of Japanese poets now writing in English to realize their poetic ideas—Fukuda Tsutomu, Nagayama Mokuo, Yaguchi Yorifumi, Nakano Michio, Nakagawa Atsuo, and many others belonging to the Poetry Society of Japan and contributing to its very interesting English-language magazine, *Poetry Nippon*.[1]

On other occasions I worked with Japanese scholars who first prepared a prose "working translation" for me, as was the case with Miyoshi Tatsuji, whom I studied and translated in this manner in collaboration with the fine literary scholar and writer Dr Fukuda Rikutarō. Poems by Satō Haruo, Murano Shirō, and many of the new women poets were translated in this way with the help of Professor Tokunaga Shōzō, himself a gifted translator of modern British and American poets.

I was fortunate also to have gained experience of working on translations of my own works into Japanese from Tokunaga Shōzō, who translated *These Horned Islands*[2] and *Japan Behind the Fan*[2] as well as many of my poems. In return, I helped him to translate Robert Lowell and many other contemporary poets. In this way too I worked with Professor Miura Fumiko who translated a large body of my poems on Japanese subjects in the bilingual collection *Japan Physical*[3], a most impressive and sensitive translation, on which we collaborated very closely. Satō Kenji, the translator of the complete works of Kathleen Raine, translated my books *A Bewick Bestiary*,[4] *Zen Gardens*,[5] and *The Body Servant*.[6] Takemoto Akiko translated my first autobiography, *The Only Child*. Through working with Japanese scholars and poets on my own work, I gained valuable experience in the art of translation.

There were many difficulties to overcome in all these varied collaborations, but none were insuperable. When the will to understand is there, one understands. I hope this volume will prove Robert Frost's slick generalization to be wrong.

It remains for me to thank, with all my heart, my many loyal and enthusiastic helpers, all old and beloved friends, and many former students, for their generous advice and support in the making of these translations. Besides assisting me in technical and practical matters, they all were able to convey to me the subtleties of various words and expressions, to elucidate obscurities, to interpret sensitively the most delicate poetic nuances. Moreover, they hunted out new and unknown poets for me, so that this volume includes work by little-known or neglected poets as well as anonymous ones. In this way I was able to present, with the devoted help of Nakano Michio, the remarkable Tsugaru dialect poems of Takagi Kyōzō and the poems of Ikeda Some and an anonymous schoolgirl ("Chewing Gum"). Similarly, Takemoto Akiko introduced me to her own discovery, an old lady who began writing poetry in her eighties, Suyama Hisayo, and to a poet-colleague at her school, Zikkoku Osamu. I discovered the outstanding qualities of the Tōhoku poet Shibuya Haruo when I first met him in Sendai in 1959, through the kind introduction of my genial colleagues there, Professors Kobayashi Atsuo and Hasegawa Matsuji. It gives me enormous pleasure and pride to present these unknown poets, more or less neglected in their own land but still imbued with the spirit of true poetry, and still writing, disregarding fame, for the sake of poetry itself, and because they have to.

My very special thanks must go to my dear friend and indefatigable correspondent, Takemoto Akiko, who helped me translate more than half the poems in this collection, for her intelligence, patience, and sensitivity, and for the sheer physical labour of writing out every poem in Japanese.

Finally, my warmest thanks go to my personal assistant of many years, Tamaki Makoto, for his practical support and advice, and his scrupulous elucidations of knotty points in many of the translations.

I should like to end this preface with a poem of my own about the art of translation which says, I hope, more than pages of prose could do.

ON THE TRANSLATION OF POETRY

Slow, passive creativity,
fluid capillary action,
the careful decanting
of old wine into other flasks—
or the transferral
not by clouds and showers
of reservoirs or lakes
into a distant city's
drought-stricken water-tanks.

The siphoning of sounds
inaudible to ordinary ear
into the receptive channels
of minds that recognize
similarities and echoes—
and a voice, no longer foreign,
close, intimate, low—
though shouting from afar,
from where all voices flow.

James Kirkup
July 1976

Notes

1. The Poetry Society of Japan, Demeure Nanzan 902, 63 Takikawa-cho, Showa-ku, Nagoya, 466, Japan.
2. Tokyo: Eichōsha,
3. Tokyo: Kenkyūsha,
4. Tokyo: Shichōsha,
5. Guildford, Surrey: Circle Press,
6. London: Dent.

Introduction
by A.R. Davis

The form of Japanese poetry defined by the word *shi* has now a span of almost a century, and Japanese literary historians and critics have long since begun to record its history and distinguish its main periods from *shintaishi* (new style *shi*) through *kindaishi* (modern *shi*) to *gendaishi* (contemporary *shi*). Though *shi* began in 1882 with translations of Western poems and its development has been continually nourished by further translations, it would be unfortunate to call it simply "Western style poetry". Equally, since modern and contemporary poetry in Japan includes new versions of the traditional *tanka* and *haiku* forms, it is difficult to equate modern Japanese poetry exclusively with *shi*. Again, while *shi* has certainly great variation of form by contrast with the general regularity of *tanka* and *haiku*, the designation "free verse" (which was indeed used in Japan during a part of its history) is not entirely applicable. In 1882, *shi* in the combination *shintaishi* (new style poems) was a convenient distinction from *tanka*, *haiku*, and *kanshi* (Chinese poems) and so it has remained until today. This anthology, then, contains mainly translations of *shi*, together with a few examples of *tanka* and *haiku*.

Shintaishi-shō (Anthology of New Style Poems, 1882), with which *shi* began, was the work of three professors of Tokyo University, Toyama Masakazu (Chuzan, 1848–1900), the founder of sociology in Japan; Yatabe Ryōkichi (Shōkon, 1852–99), a botanist who introduced Darwinism to Japan; and Inoue Tetsujirō (Sonken, 1855–1944), who became the first Japanese professor of philosophy. It contained fourteen translations of Western poems and five original pieces. The poems translated were: "The Soldier's Return" by Robert Bloomfield (1766–1823); "Ye Mariners of England" by Thomas Campbell

(1777–1844); "The Charge of the Light Brigade" by Alfred Tennyson (1809–92); "Elegy Written in a Country Churchyard" by Thomas Gray (1716–71); "A Psalm of Life" by Henry Wadsworth Longfellow (1807–82) in two versions; "The Revenge" by Tennyson; "The Three Fishers" by Charles Kingsley (1819–75); Wolsey's speech ("Farewell! a long farewell, to all my greatness!") from Shakespeare's *Henry VIII*, act 3, scene 2; "Ballade" ("Bien moustrez, printemps gracieux") by Charles d'Orléans (1394–1465), "Children" by Longfellow; the "O sleep! O gentle sleep!" speech from Shakespeare's *Henry IV*, part 2, act 3, scene 1, and the "To be, or not to be" speech from *Hamlet*, act 3, scene 1.

"Meiji poems should be Meiji poems and not old poems; Japanese poetry should be Japanese poetry and not Chinese poetry. That is why we are writing new style poems" (Inoue's preface to his translation of Longfellow's "A Psalm of Life"). The high seriousness of the authors' purpose was mocked by the strangeness of its execution, which has been criticized as "crude" and "ludicrous". Yet such was the power of a first step in the Meiji period and so great was the energy with which a beginning was followed up that within twenty years new style poems of enduring merit had been written.

The importance of *Shintaishi-shō* lay in its self-consciousness. A new *Japanese* poetry was to be deliberately sought, and the path to modernity and nationalism was to be pursued through the translation and adaptation of the poetry of the West. The apparent contradictions, such as the very Chinese-looking title of Yatabe's translation of Gray's Elegy, "Funjō Kankai" (Thoughts upon a Tomb) and the very traditional seven-five-syllable rhythm of the translations, were inevitable and were to prove difficult of resolution. Yatabe could lament that the use of everyday language had been rare in previous Japanese poetry, but while translation of Western poetry and the introduction of its topics could serve to effect a break with the highly conventional subject-matter and diction of traditional poetry, it could not directly solve the problem of a Japanese language and form in which non-traditional subjects might be treated. Language reform and the language to be used in literature were in fact general issues in Meiji Japan, raised by the drive towards nationalism and modernization, which inevitably included the requirement of general education. This historical context explains why the first step towards a new poetry came from reformers seeking to change society and culture rather than from poets.

This first anthology established a vogue in the following decade for *shintaishi*. The subjects of these were still often as strange as Toyama Masakazu's "On the Principles of Sociology" in *Shintaishi-shō*, but being the work of poets, they showed greater linguistic sensitivity. Nevertheless, it was a volume composed entirely of translations which carried the movement towards its first success. *Omokage* (Vestiges; original title *Moshiogusa*, Seaweed) appeared first in 1889 in a supplement to the magazine *Kokumin no Tomo* (The Nation's Friend). The five translators went under the name of Shinseisha (New Voices Society) and included Mori Ōgai (1862–1922), whose life embraced both medicine in the Imperial Japanese Army and letters as translator, creative writer, and literary theorist, and Ochiai Naobumi (1861–1903), who subsequently became best known as a leader in the reformation of the traditional thirty-one-syllable *tanka* poem, but who at this time had gained wide acclaim for a long poem which had been set to music, "Kōjo Shiragiku no Uta" (Song of the Filial Daughter White Chrysanthemum).[1]

Omokage has no preface proclaiming its principles, only lines from the earliest collection of Japanese poetry, the *Manyōshu* and from the Chinese poet Su Tung-p'o (1037–1101) as epigraphs. These indicate the departure of its contents from the path followed by the authors of *Shintaishi-shō*. The language is elegantly classical, and some of the translations are into Chinese. Yet the high literary quality achieved in these translations of Shakespeare and Byron, Goethe, Heine, and other German poets, as well as of Chinese and early Japanese originals was of importance in the establishment of new poetry.

Ōgai's Japanese translation of Manfred's opening speech and his Chinese translation of the Invocation in Byron's dramatic poem may not have directly influenced Kitamura Tōkoku (1868 –94) whose "Hōraikyoku" (Song of Paradise) can be seen to owe much to "Manfred", since Tōkoku probably read the poem in the original. Yet they are equally manifestations of the Japanese discovery of romanticism in the third decade of Meiji (1887–96). Tōkoku is generally regarded as the pioneer romantic, but he ended his short life by suicide in 1894. In that year, together with Shimazaki Tōson² and other young Japanese, he had founded the magazine *Bungakkai*, which for the years of its existence, 1894–98, was central in the expression of Japanese romanticism. Romanticism was the spirit that imbued the volume of new poetry which is accepted as marking its maturity as a literary form, *Wakana-shū* (Young Herbs, 1897) by Tōkoku's friend Shimazaki Tōson.

It has become something of a cliché in studies of Meiji history to see the third decade as a period of growing alienation of liberal intellectuals from the modernizing bureaucratic state, and the literary evidence is powerful in support of this view. Yet while sociological forces press heavily upon literature, it has always generative powers within itself. Romanticism certainly answered the rebellious mood of the young of the 1890s, but the literature of European romanticism also provided for them a belief in literature as a serious pursuit of life. "Life is force; force is utterance; utterance is words; new words are thus new life", wrote Tōson in the preface to his collected poems (1904).

Tōson did not stay long upon the poetry scene but left it to seek his "new life" in the novel. For he had not solved the linguistic problem posed by new poetry and had himself become conscious of its confinement of expression. Tōson's poems are a peak of achievement, but they did not point a way forward. This was to come from other directions. It is indeed difficult, even with the simplification of concentration upon the most significant features, to trace the progress of new poetry through the fourth decade of Meiji (1897–1906) entirely in the semblance of a straight line. In Meiji Japan, where the tides from the West swept in with a remarkably short interval between, European literary movements separated by several decades might be introduced within a few years. Thus the Meiji forties embraced both romanticism and naturalism. Since the two occurred within so short a time and often within the work of one writer, it is obviously impossible to see them in violent opposition to each other. Both have been seen as serving to establish the individualism of the writer against the oppressive power of society. In this way it seems possible to understand the transition of Tōson from writing poetry under the influence of Wordsworth and Shelley to novels under that of Dostoevsky.

The current that carried new poetry through the early years of the twentieth century, however, must initially be characterized as romantic. Yosano Tekkan (1873–1935), who in 1900 founded the New Poetry Society and its magazine *Myōjō* (Bright Star), was more successful as a *tanka* than a *shi* poet, and as a *tanka* poet he was surpassed by his wife, Yosano Akiko. Akiko's romantic poems on their love may be the chief glory of *Myōjō*, but the achievement of her husband, who edited the magazine through a hundred numbers, is not to be belittled. *Myōjō* was one of the most influential magazines of the period and the nursery of the poets who carried new poetry into the Taishō era (1912–26), in particular, Ishikawa Takuboku, Kitahara Hakushū, and Takamura Kōtarō. The nine years of its existence may be divided into three periods. The first was 1900–1902, when the magazine was centred chiefly on the reformed *tanka* (i.e., the traditional poem written with a consciousness of Western literature and modern ideas) of Tekkan and Akiko and their followers. The magazine never ceased to give prominence to *tanka*, but in its second period until 1906 many examples of *shi* appear as well as the translations of symbolist poetry by Ueda Bin (1874–1916), which were to exert so far-reaching an effect on modern Japanese poetry.

From the point of view of their origins, symbolism and naturalism—of which the rise is seen as a factor in the decline of *Myōjō* in its third and last period (1907–8), are out of sequence in Japan. Yet Japanese writers were treating their introductions of Western literary ideas in terms of their own psychological needs, and their instinct was essentially synthetic (hence the seemingly strange appearance of "Naturalistic Symbolism" in critical discussions of the time). Tekkan did not aid the declining fortunes of *Myōjō* by an anti-naturalist declaration. Nor did the expedition of *Myōjō* poets to Kyūshū in 1907 save it. Instead, this tour of the remains of Japan's "Christian Century", the Nanban (Southern Barbarian) period of the sixteenth-seventeenth centuries, provided Kinoshita Mokutarō and Kitahara Hakushū with exotic subject matter with which to meet the *fin de siecle* "decadent" feeling which duly arose as the Meiji era came to an end.

Still the problem of form and language remained, and it seemed that Meiji would end without any significant move towards a language of everyday speech which the pioneers had thought important. Classicism was strong in the translations of Ueda Bin, both in form and in language, for all that *Kaichō-on* (Sound of the Western Seas, 1905), the volume in which his earliest translations of French symbolist poetry were collected, remains one of the acknowledged masterpieces of modern Japanese poetry. The first Japanese symbolist poets, Kanbara Ariake (1876–1952) and Susukida Kyūkin (1877–1945), who both published volumes in 1906, equally tended towards classicism and to an archaicism in expression. Symbolism had an endemic appeal for Japanese, who had always valued suggestion, and it continually carried the danger of turning into a lifeless aestheticism.

Appearing at the moment of the onset of naturalism in the Japanese literary world, the first symbolists attracted critics as well as followers. Now for the first time there was a determined call for the use of colloquial language, a realistic treatment and the abandonment of traditional poetic forms. Rather than in its earliest experimental works this movement found its greatest strength in the outstanding naturalist critic Shimamura Hōgetsu (1871–1918), whose articles provided an important theoretical foundation for the development of free verse in the colloquial language. Although a Free Verse Society (Jiyūshisha) was founded in 1909 and numbered Yamamura Bochō among its early members, success had generally to wait for the new Taishō era. Meiji was still to end with a last version of romanticism, in which French symbolism had its share, with the "decadents" of the Pan Society, named after the Greek god of music and pleasure.

The Pan Society, founded in December 1908, brought together young Meiji Western-style painters like Ishii Hakutei (1882–1958) and Yamamoto Kanae (1882–1946) and poets of the just-ended *Myōjō* like Kinoshita Mokutarō and Kitahara Hakushū in a symposium which first met at a Western restaurant near the Ryōgoku Bridge in Tokyo. In the next years its membership increased to include novelists and other writers and it became virtually *de rigueur* for anyone who aspired to a name in letters in the capital to belong. The gatherings became large, noisy, and ostentatious. For the past thirty years young Japanese with a passionate enthusiasm and an incredible skill had introduced the literature, art, and thought of the West. The risk of a loss of sincerity must always have been present, and it is remarkable that they so seldom fell victim. Perhaps here in the

Pan Society the too theatrical attempt at adoption of foreign attitudes was one occasion. Even so, with a poet like Kinoshita Mokutarō the stance of ennui could transcend affectation and express a modern sensibility.

The transition from new poetry to modern poetry in these years had been primarily a literary and individualist phenomenon. New Poetry had begun in a feeling of the limitation of traditional forms and in an excitement over the greater expressiveness of discovered Western poetry. Western poetry and Western literature, together with Christianity, made young Japanese conscious of the oppressiveness of their society and seemed to offer a way of life in opposition to it. At the same time, the traditional literary heritage proved stronger than imagined. *Tanka* and *haiku* could accommodate Western approaches to life, as is witnessed by the romantic love poetry of Yosano Akiko and the despairing realism of Ishikawa Takuboku. Traditional literary language and rhythms often seemed likely to dominate the *shi* poem. In these thirty years, poetry was relatively little thought of as an ideological vehicle for political and social change, but there are a few commonly noted examples such as *Shakaishugi-shishū* (Collection of Socialist Poetry) by Kodama Kagai (1874–1943), which was banned after its publication in 1903 and especially Takuboku's final shift towards socialism at the end of his brief life under the influence of the trial for treason of Kōtoku Shūsui (1871–1911) and other socialists in 1910.

The Taishō period (1912–26) brought to full development the tendencies that had emerged in the last years of Meiji: the movement for free verse and colloquial language and a concern with social and political problems. At the same time classicism and aestheticism did not wholly surrender the field. There was indeed an increasing tendency towards a diversity in which opposing and divergent trends existed side by side. The introduction of Western poetry and of Western theories was steadily pursued, and the time interval between Japanese poetic movements and their foreign sources had by the end of the period been virtually eliminated. Japan had caught up and could share in *avant-garde* ideas. In its achievement of modernity and contemporaneity poetry moved from *kindaishi* to *gendaishi*.

When Taishō began, the twin pillars of the new-poetry world were Kitahara Hakushū and Miki Rofū, both symbolists but of a considerably different tone. Rofū's poetry has a tranquillity and a wistful melancholy which contrasts with Hakushū's early exuberance and extravagance. The two poets published together in a special number of the magazine *Zanboa* in 1912. Rofū's contributions, reprinted in 1913 in his fourth volume *Shiroki Te no Karyūdo* (The White-handed Huntsman), are regarded as the peak of his achievement. His symbolism had been influenced by the translations by Nagai Kafū (1879–1959) of Henri de Régnier, Verlaine, and Baudelaire, published in magazines from 1909 and brought together in *Sango-shū* (Coral Anthology) in 1913, a collection which is ranked next to Ueda Bin's *Kaichō-on*.

Although Rofū had been one of the early experimenters with colloquial language, he had afterwards returned to the literary style. Takamura Kōtarō, however, who had returned from his studies of art in Europe to join in the "decadence" of the Pan Society, moved in early Taishō towards the humanism of the *Shirakaba* (White Birch) group, which became a great force in Taishō literature. In his collection *Dōtei* (Journey, 1914) he produced one of the first major works in free verse and colloquial language. The adherence of the three other major poets to emerge in the early years of Taishō—Murō Saisei, Hagiwara Sakutarō, and Yamamura Bochō—secured the success of the colloquial style.

Colloquialism and a desire for simplicity went hand in hand with humanism and social concern. Japan was affected by the world currents towards democracy aroused by the world war. "Democratic" poets like Walt Whitman, Horace Traubel, and

Edward Carpenter were introduced at this time. *Leaves of Grass* was translated by Arishima Takeo (1878–1923), a leading member of the *Shirakaba* group, Traubel's poems were translated by Fukuda Masao (1893–1952), and Carpenter's by Tomita Saika (b. 1890). Fukuda and Tomita were both poets of the Minshū-shi (Popular Poetry) group, which flourished 1917–25 and published *Minshū* (The People, January–October 1918) and other magazines. In 1922 this group produced an *Anthology of Japanese Socialist Poets* and an *Anthology of Western Socialist Poets* in translation. The group is historically noteworthy for its contribution to the development of colloquial poetry and for its introduction of the lives and work of the masses into Japanese poetry. Yet none of its leading members—Fukuda, Tomita, Shiratori Shōgo (1890–1973), or Momota Sōji (1893–1955)—achieved the first rank among modern poets, and their concern with a popular content was heavily attacked by poets of essentially diverse mentality like Kitahara Hakushū and Hagiwara Sakutarō, who were united in their view of the importance of poetic artistry and lyrical expression.

The opposition between the two groups split the contemporary poetry world, which had united in the foundation of a Shiwakai (Poetry Discussion Association) in 1917. The Shiwakai published eight annual anthologies (*Nihon Shishū*) from 1917 on as well as a number of other representative collections. After the split in 1921, Kitahara Hakushū, Miki Rofū, and other leading members resigned and left the Shiwakai for its remaining five years until its dissolution in October 1926 in the hands of the Popular Poetry group. The dissidents formed a Shinshikai (New Poetry Association) and started a rival anthology series (*Gendai Shishū*) but achieved only one volume.

The Popular Poetry group may certainly be regarded as a manifestation of the spirit of the times, and as Japan moved into the 1920s and a general movement for proletarian literature, backed by the establishment of the Japan Socialist League

(December 1920), arose, its members might well have seen themselves in a leading role. In fact, they were to be attacked by some of the advocates of proletarian literature no less fiercely than they had earlier been by the lyric poets. In the 1910s also, a far greater significance in the history of modern poetry belongs to the *Kanjō* group, which arose with the inauguration of the magazine *Kanjō* (Feelings) in June 1916 by Murō Saisei and Hagiwara Sakutarō. The association of these two poets was based on personal friendship which ignored a considerable difference of background and had no shared social or political ideology. Personal friendship has certainly been important in the coteries of modern poetry, but more generally they have had their basis in attendance at the same schools and universities. *Kanjō* ran for thirty-two issues up to November 1919. Besides Murō and Hagiwara, the most important contributor was Yamamura Bochō, although he moved away after 1917 (the three poets had earlier been associated in a *Ningyo Shisha*, Mermaid Poetry Society).

Yamamura, even though he soon became affected by a strongly humanistic tendency, was at first an experimentalist with imagist techniques and may be regarded as an early example of the *avant-garde* stance. Murō's poetry also had a humanistic strain which was different in quality from that of the young aristocrats of the *Shirakaba* group and of the Popular Poetry group. His friend Hagiwara expressed the greatest admiration for Murō's success in capturing for the first time in the colloquial verse movement a deeply emotive and truly Japanese rhythm. Murō's maiden work, *Ai no Shishū* (Poems of Love), enjoyed an immediate popularity and became one of the classics of modern poetry. Hagiwara's praise of his friend indicates the direction of his own quest: the forming of a language stripped of florid or shallowly loquacious diction as a vehicle for personal expression. The intensity of Hagiwara's solitariness made him deny in his verse and his criticism any other aim for poetry than lyricism. He was violently opposed to the class standpoint of the Proletarian Literature movement. His achievement in words and rhythm justifies his own recognition of his *Tsuki ni Hoeru* (Baying the Moon, 1917) as the seminal volume of the period. Though Hagiwara's influence was of such importance and though he was at the centre of the *Kanjō* group which included some number of good poets, he was essentially not a man for the slogans and movements which were to characterize the 1920s and early 1930s.

As in Europe, an artistic *avant-garde* shaded into an ideological movement. Futurism and Dadaism with an admixture of anarchism and socialism carried some through a revolution in art to social revolutionary literature, while others continued the pursuit of modernity in art until finally nationalistic demands, as Japan came to the Pacific War, forced all to silence or patriotic conformity.

Hirado Renkichi (1893–1922) led off with the "First Manifesto of the Japan Futurists Movement" in 1921, followed by Takahashi Shinkichi, who has been an enduring figure in poetry and art, with his "Dadaist Manifesto" in 1922. January 1923 saw the foundation of the short-lived, slim, yet important coterie magazine *Aka to Kuro* (Red and Black) by the Dadaist Hagiwara Kyōjirō (1899–1938), together with Tsuboi Shigeji (1898–1975), Okamoto Jun (b. 1901), both of whom were to be prominent in the Proletarian Literature movement. *Aka to Kuro* in its opening manifesto rejected existing tradition, authority, and order. Poems were to be bombs in the hands of these anarchist poets; against the humanist poets of the Popular Poetry group they declared their fierce enmity. *Aka to Kuro* thus expressed the spirit of revolt which had come into poetry in an especially violent manner.

An *avant-garde* magazine which achieved a much longer life (almost four years as against *Aka to Kuro*'s year and a half) was *A*, which was launched in January 1924 outside the mainland of

Japan in Dairen (the Chinese city of Ta-lien which with Port Arthur the Japanese had gained from the Russians in 1905). Its founders were Kitagawa Fuyuhiko, Anzai Fuyue (1898–1965), who was the editor in Dairen, and others. Kitagawa has throughout a long life remained a foremost promoter of significant poetry magazines. Notable among *A*'s subsequent contributions were Miyoshi Tatsuji and Haruyama Yukio (b. 1902). The *A* poets were proponents of a new short poem and of a new style of prose-poetry. In both they aimed at condensed expression with an instant impact. Here they exemplified the ambiguity of the title of their magazine, which might stand for "Asia", with its emphasis on brevity in poetic expression, or for an "Ah!" of startled surprise. In their revolution in the forms of modern Japanese poetry, the *A* poets were seeking the recovery of a poetic spirit which they believed to have been lost.

A was the immediate forerunner of *Shi to Shiron* (Poetry and Poetics), a quarterly which ran from September 1928 until December 1931. *Shi to Shiron* for the years of its existence was the central organ of Japanese modernist poets. It was the culmination of the *avant-garde* trend of the 1920s and the origin of all subsequent *avant-garde* movements. Every post-war European modernist movement and poet found mention and consideration in its pages. Its founding members included Kitagawa Fuyuhiko, Anzai Fuyue, Miyoshi Tatsuji, and Haruyama Yukio from *A*, which had ceased publication a year earlier. Haruyama became editor and established himself as the magazine's leading theorist. He was joined in the advocacy of surrealism by Nishiwaki Junzaburō, who had thus far published poetry in English but who was about to emerge as a major figure in contemporary Japanese poetry. Once again, a major new poetic movement was promoted by an outstanding work of translation; the work in question was Horiguchi Daigaku's *Gekka no Ichigun* (A Herd in the Moonlight), a volume of translations of contemporary French poets, published in 1925.

The great emphasis on theory in *Shi to Shiron* was characteristic of the early years of the Shōwa era (1926–). In the same period the Proletarian Literature movement, to which *Shi to Shiron* with its concept of "pure poetry" stood in direct opposition, went through many organizational shifts and gave great place to theoretical discussion. Poetry was only one of the arts to which the ideological reformers gave their attention, but even quantitatively it occupied an important place in the movement. There were ten or more left-wing coterie magazines which were amalgamated to produce *Proletarian Poetry* as the organ of the Proletarian Poets Association in 1931, and the association numbered about ninety poets in its ranks. A large number of individual collections and anthologies were published by poets who adhered to the movement and whose names, apart from those of Nakano Shigeharu and a few others, are little remembered outside the pages of literary histories.

While the 1920s had been a significant period of revolt, either artistic or social, and historical emphasis properly falls upon this, avant-gardism and proletarianism do not tell its whole story. In 1927 there was a fresh attempt to create a general body for poets for the first time since the break-up of the Shiwakai in 1921. Though this new Shijin Kyōkai (Poets Society) gathered some two hundred members, it was dissolved in 1928 just after it had published a 1928 Poets' Yearbook (*Shijin Nenkan*). This work reveals in a survey for 1927 the existence of 180 poetry magazines throughout Japan, and this may give an idea of the diversity of poetic effort at this time.

The sorting hand of time has after half a century consigned most of these magazines and their contributors to obscurity. One, however, which the increasing fame of its founder and some of its contributors through these fifty years has raised above its original standing, is *Dora* (Gong). Founded by Kusano Shinpei in April 1925, *Dora* survived for four years with sixteen issues. It included among its contributors Miyazawa Kenji, Takamura

Kōtarō, Takahashi Shinkichi, and Ono Tōzaburō. Kusano and his magazine may be and are classified as anarchist, but an anarchism which could embrace the scientific agriculturalist Miyazawa, who worked for the well-being of his remote northern farming community, and the critical humanist Takamura could not be of a violent political kind. It was above all a strong individualism, coupled with a profound love of humanity and Nature, which was the unifying characteristic of this group. *Dora* was Kusano's first attempt at magazine publishing which led him through a number of successors to the enduring *Rekitei* (The Course of History, 1935–).

His immediate recognition of Miyazawa Kenji was a great tribute to Kusano's literary judgment (he was twenty-two at the time). For Miyazawa, like himself, was at this time very much an outsider in terms of the Tokyo-centred world. Another outsider of another sort, since he was a refugee from the centre rather than a dweller upon the periphery, Kaneko Mitsuharu, had achieved his first success slightly earlier in 1923. Kaneko, who died in 1975 and whose collected works are now appearing in a fine edition, decorated with the emblem of the *kogane-mushi* (gold bug) which gave the title to his 1923 collection, has been in his consistency through the pre-war and post-war periods the salvation of the Japanese poetic conscience. For Kaneko virtually alone continued in an unswerving resistance to nationalism and imperialism.

For the Japanese poetry world the Manchurian Incident of 1931, by which Japan deprived China of her Manchurian provinces and created the puppet state of Manchukuo, marks a significant, if not a precise, dividing point to which the post-war generation had to a great extent to return to make a new beginning. It was of course ten years before Japan entered into the Pacific War, but the decade 1931–41 shows a gradual loss of collective impulse, and what was new turned out at best as some preparation for the post-war period. The greatest check fell upon the members of the Proletarian Literature movement, who were forced by government pressure not only into organizational dissolution (1934) but into individual recantation.

The *avant-garde* theorists of *Shi to Shiron* were less subject to political pressure than their Proletarian Literature rivals, although as ultra-nationalism mounted, it brought opposition to cosmopolitanism and suspicion of manifestations of an international spirit. The ending of *Shi to Shiron* came rather through internal divisions. The first important defectors were Kitagawa Fuyuhiko and Miyoshi Tatsuji, who joined with others in the publication of a new quarterly, *Shi, Genjitsu* (Poetry and Reality), which achieved five issues between June 1930 and June 1931. *Shi, Genjitsu*, together with the first series of the monthly *Jikan* (Time), which, again under Kitagawa's leadership, produced twelve issues in roughly the same period, marks the beginning of the neo-realist movement which came into prominence in the post-war period when Kitagawa edited the second *Jikan* (1950–). While Kitagawa and Miyoshi were united in opposition to surrealism, their political positions were beginning to diverge. Kitagawa moved further to the Left and joined the Proletarians, while Miyoshi with his friend Maruyama Kaoru, who had also become a contributor to *Shi, Genjitsu* and *Jikan*, were to become with Hori Tatsuo (1904–53) editors of the lyricist and politically conservative *Shiki* (Four Seasons). *Shiki* began as a quarterly for two issues (May and July) in 1933 and then ran as a monthly from October 1934 to June 1944. Miyoshi and Maruyama (the latter slightly older and outliving his friend by ten years) provide a comparison which may afford a sidelight on the situation of modern Japanese poetry. Many would accord Miyoshi the foremost place in twentieth-century poetry. Yet it is a fact that the last of Miyoshi's volumes of poems appeared in 1952, a dozen years before his death, whereas Maruyama continued to publish and continually "modernized" his sea-poems until almost the end of his life. That Miyoshi's work became increasingly "classical" has a note of complaint, when seen against an always moving standard of "modernity". His cessation of publication after 1952 may have been a personal recognition of having fallen behind this moving standard. Yet his poetry deserves to be seen as a superb synthesis of the Sino-Japanese tradition with the introduced rhythms and expression of the West. *Shiki* was a reaction against the extreme intellectualism and modernism of *Shi to Shiron* towards a lyric poetry which modulated intellect and emotion. It brought together the older Taishō lyric poets, Hagiwara Sakutarō, Murō Saisei, Satō Haruo, Horiguchi Daigaku, and young men like Nakahara Chūya and Tachihara Michizō (1914–39) with Miyoshi, Maruyama, Takenaka Iku, and others who had appeared in the 1920s as a middle generation.

The line of the *avant-garde* did not die out with *Shi to Shiron* but may be traced up to 1941 through a number of successors. The banner of surrealism and the *avant-garde* was directly taken up by Kitasono Katsue (b. 1902), and apart from the years of the Pacific War he did not surrender it. His editorial path must, however, be followed through occasionally different titles, of which *VOU* is the most enduring and the best known. Before the first series of *VOU* (July 1935–October 1940) came *Madame Blanche* (May 1932–August 1934); the gap in the post-war run of *VOU* (revived in December 1946) was filled by *Cendre*. In the first series of *VOU*, together with Nishiwaki Junzaburō and Murano Shirō, who were becoming established leaders, the names of Tamura Ryūichi and Ayukawa Nobuo made their first appearance. Inside a hardening nationalism, Kitasono asserted his faith in the "unique current of the *avant-garde* throughout the whole world". As a further illustration of the same faith, there appeared in 1937, the year when war with China became widespread, a new *avant-garde* magazine *Shin-ryōdo* (New Territory) which echoed the title of Michael Roberts's anthology of contemporary English poetry, *New Country*. *Shin-ryōdo*, in which Murano Shirō collaborated with former *Shi to Shiron* members like Haruyama Yukio, survived until January 1942. The fleeting appearance of *Arechi* (Waste Land) which was to become so prominent a part of the early post-war scene, in March 1939 is also to be noted. We have thus traced all the five heads of what Kitasono Katsue, writing in 1954, called the 'five-headed dragon'' of contemporary Japanese poetry—his own *VOU* group, the *Arechi* group, the poets of Kitagawa Fuyuhiko's *Jikan*, of Kusano Shinpei's *Rekitei*, and the successors of the Proletarians—in the 1930s, but the Pacific War, when it finally came, cut the history of modern poetry in two. Japanese historians are largely silent about the intervening years, and the established poets who remained silent in those years are fortunate. For some like Takamura Kōtarō, who was especially vocal in the general and surely understandable patriotism of the time, the war years cannot escape being a misfortune. Yet Takamura survived the misfortune of a loss of reputation and of material loss in the bombing of Tokyo to write more good poetry in his last decade and to find continuing critical acclaim since his death in 1956. Perhaps, too, one may see in a long view Hiroshima and the Japanese sufferings of the early post-war period as softening any guilt that may be felt for the nationalistic excesses of writers during the war.

The arising of Japanese poetry from the devastation of the lost war was remarkably rapid. Within two years of its ending many established pre-war poets had published new volumes, old magazines had been restarted and new magazines begun. The Proletarian Literature writers, who had been forced to dissolve their organization eleven years earlier, were as a movement first in the field. By the end of 1945 they had organized *Shin-Nihon Bungaku* (Literature of New Japan), headed by a celebrated article by the radical woman-writer Miyamoto Yuriko (1889–1951), *Utagoe yo Okore* (Singing Voices, Arise!).

The New Japan Literary Society replaced "proletarian" by "democratic" in its aims and sought—and to some extent initially succeeded in attracting—a membership from a wider political spectrum. As in the past, it gave great place to the "enhancing and concentration of the creative literary energies of the mass of the people". As a result there was a considerable development of literary circles and poetry circles among industrial and rural workers. A notable example commonly cited for the immediate post-war period is the Kokutetsu Shijin Renmei (National Railways Poets League), organized by Kondō Azuma (b. 1904), who had been earlier a leading member of *Shi to Shiron*. These workers' poetry circles have been but one factor in the enormous spread of poetry writing and poetry-magazine production throughout post-war Japan. As in their earlier Proletarian Literature days, the writers of the Left set great emphasis on organization, and there was once again considerable controversy and factionalism. In the early post-war period there was a fierce "generation controversy" between the older writers who had undergone "conversion" and the younger writers whom age had saved from compromise. The Proletarian Literature past and the war years long continued as a source of conflict within the New Japan Literary Society, which, however, remained the major force in left-wing literature.

Yet the group which most especially represents the first post-war decade was that of the *Arechi* (Waste Land) poets, Ayukawa Nobuo, Miyoshi Toyoichirō, Tamura Ryūichi, Kuroda Saburō, Nakagiri Masao, Kitamura Tarō, and Kihara Kōichi (Takano Kikuo and Yoshimoto Takaaki, b. 1924, were later adherents). They took their name from T.S. Eliot's 1922 poem and they were conscious of their debt to him, but they were perhaps nearer to the existentialism of Sartre and Camus. In the famous "Dedication to X" (*X e no Kenji*), printed at the beginning of the first *Arechi* anthology (1951), their faith was declared: "The escape from destruction, the protest against ruin are our will to rebel against our own fate and are also testimony to our existence. If there is to be a future for us and for you, it depends on our not despairing of our present life." The *Arechi* poets were all men in their twenties, who had had experience in the war which imposed its burden upon them. In the contemporary wasteland of Japan, where all previous authority had fallen in ruins, they utterly rejected the past. They were a group which had mainly formed personal relationships in the late 1930s when the first *Arechi* had briefly appeared, but they were unable to revive the magazine until September 1947. Even then it continued only until June 1948; the main effort of the group came through the series of (nearly) annual anthologies, published between 1951 and 1958. The *Arechi* poets were above all a group of individualists (all continued as important figures in contemporary poetry after the *Arechi* period was over) for whom the "socialist", "lyricist", or "intellectualist" labels which other contemporary groups bore were unfitting.

By the time of the Korean War, Kitasono Katsue's *VOU* group (1946), Kusano Shinpei's *Rekitei* (1947) and Kitagawa Fuyuhiko's *Jikan* (1950) had revived, and together with these enduring elements of the poetry scene, a new general association of poets without any concern for ideological commitment, the Japan Modern Poets Society (Nihon Gendai Shijin Kai) had been established (December 1949). A poetry magazine which equally sought to be a general organ of the Japanese poetry world, *Utopia*, had been launched by Jō Samon (b. 1904), Akiya Yutaka (b. 1922), and others in September 1946. Renamed *Shigaku* (Poetry Studies) in 1947, it has persisted to the present day.

The first real challenge, however, to parity with the *Arechi* group in the leadership of the post-war generation came with the formation of *Rettō* (the magazine ran from March 1952 until October 1955). The *Rettō* poets, who advocated a documentary realism, largely succeeded in breaking out of the typical theoretical techniques of left-wing poetry and looking at actual society with a clear vision. They caught the imagination of readers in a Japan where the devastation of the war was beginning to disappear, the Occupation had ended, and where independence and with it a sense of the dangers of the outside world were returning. The protest poetry of Louis Aragon and Paul Eluard enjoyed a vogue, and the A-bomb poems of Hara Tamiki (1905–51) and Tōge Sankichi were well known. The leading poets of *Rettō* were Sekine Hiroshi (b. 1920), Hasegawa Ryūsei, and Kuroda Kio (the last with his unusual element of fantasy hardly fulfilled Sekine's prescription of documentary realism). They demonstrated once again that poetry of ideological commitment could succeed if married to poetic ability.

In stressing the place of the *Rettō* poets in the first half of the 1950s, the continued presence upon the scene of the major poets of the "artistic" opposition, above all Nishiwaki Junzaburō and Murano Shirō, must not be neglected. In the month after *Rettō* made its appearance, Nishiwaki and Murano with Kitasono Katsue and Andō Ichirō (b. 1907) launched a new magazine, *Gala* (*VOU* was of course still continuing). At the same time, there was the appearance of what has been called the quasi-post-war generation in the notable person of Tanikawa Shuntarō, who entered the poetry world with the recommendation of Miyoshi Tatsuji. Tanikawa's *Nijū Oku Kōnen no Kodoku* (The Loneliness of Twenty Million Light Years, 1952) showed for the first time a poet who had escaped the wounds of the war.

In 1953 Tanikawa joined with other young poets, Kawasaki Hiroshi (b. 1930), Ibaragi Noriko, Ōoka Makoto, and Yoshino Hiroshi, all of whom were in their twenties, in founding *Kai* (Oar). In comparison with the *Arechi* and *Rettō* poets, the *Kai* group showed a sense of tradition and locality. They were above all lyric poets with an intellectual tendency. *Kai* was a Tokyo but not a university group. Yet its example was quickly emulated in *Han* (Overflowing), founded by Horikawa Masami and other

Waseda students in June 1953 and in *Baku* (Tapir) by Meiji students in December; in July of the following year Keiō students launched *Suna* (Sand). All contributed to the appearance of a new lyric poetry. These young poets also tended to stand apart from the bitter controversies that raged in the years 1954–55 between the socialist and aesthetic camps of the poetry world and also within the left itself.

The position of the socialist side was strengthened by the inauguration of the magazine *Gendaishi* (Contemporary Poetry) in July 1954 as an official organ of the New Japan Literary Society.[3] Veteran leftists like Okamoto Jun, Tsuboi Shigeji, and Kaneko Mitsuharu were joined in *Gendaishi* by the young men of the *Rettō* group. On the other wing of the poetry scene an event of future significance was the foundation in 1955 of the Surrealist Study Society by Iijima Kōichi (b. 1930), Ōoka Makoto and others.

The second half of the 1950s saw the beginnings of a new prosperity in Japan, which was to change the living standards and life-style of the general public. The transistor and the television set became universal, and weekly magazines boomed (the ruin of literature was confidently predicted). The economic horizons of poetry also were enlarged, and the *Kai* poets in particular, though others also, turned to the writing of poetical drama and *chansons* for the mass media. Tanikawa Shuntarō, who had made clear his quest for a large audience in *Sekai e* (To the World, 1956), more than anyone else created a new image of the poet as a widely known figure who rode in his own motor car. An indication of the widening audience may be seen in the appearance of the commercial poetry magazines, *Eureka* (October 1956), *Mugen* (Infinity), edited by Kitagawa Fuyuhiko, Kusano Shinpei, and Murano Shirō (May 1959), and *Gendaishi Techō* (Contemporary Poetry Notebook, June 1959).

American and British influences began for the first time (if one excludes Eliot) for fifty years and more to have a major effect on poetry with the introduction of American beat-poetry and the attitudes of Britain's "Angry Young Men". The work of the Surrealist Study Society was also, nonetheless, taking hold, and *Wani* (Crocodile; ran July 1959–September 1962), founded by Yoshioka Minoru, Kiyooka Takayuki (b. 1922), Iijima Kōichi, Ōoka Makoto, and Iwata Hiroshi, advocated a new surrealist poetry. While the poets of the Left continued to argue over poets' social responsibilities (this was the period of agitation against the revision of the Security Treaty with the United States, which is a major dividing line in the poetical and intellectual history of post-war Japan), a wider questioning of the nature and aims of poetry arose within poetry circles, and at the same time some notable attacks on contemporary poetry came from distinguished critics who were not poets.

When one attempts to carry the history of *shi*-poetry through the 1960s and into the 1970s, one's sources in Japanese standardized literary history begin to fail—everywhere literary history is liable to fall a generation behind the present—and the task for the limited competence of the foreign observer becomes yet more difficult. In the last ten years it has indeed become easier to know about the pre-1960 and still more the pre-1945 history of *shi*. For there has been a poetry "boom" which has produced collected works of the major older poets, large collections of modern and contemporary poetry, facsimile reprints of magazines such as *Myōjō* and *Shiki*, and many studies of modern poetry and individual poets. Although greater effort, particularly by the large publishing houses that do not specialize in poetry, has been given to the established figures of the past, some post-war poets have also achieved selected or collected works, and the leading poetry publisher Shichōsha has a continuing library of individual contemporary poets, which has at the time of writing reached sixty-five volumes. The commercial poetry magazines (including *Eureka*, which died in the early 1960s and has now been revived) are flourishing, along with the numerous coterie and local magazines. Poetry has certainly shared in Japanese affluence and has perhaps come a little too close to being institutionalized. The number of annual poetry prizes has grown since the Mr H. Prize was first awarded in 1951; Takamura Kōtarō, Murō Saisei, and others have since been commemorated in annual awards. Thus many poets can be elevated to the order of prize-winners. The gaining of one of these prizes has indeed become an expected entry in a poet's biographical outline. The excuse for writing poetry—"because I have nothing else to do" —which Tomioka Taeko claims that she invented on account of its being impossible to say she was doing it for a living, risks becoming outdated. Not many poets as yet may make such a living, but the process of becoming "established" appears to be being continuously shortened. The poets of the "pure" post-war generation—Amazawa Taijirō (b. 1936), Watanabe Takenobu (b. 1938), Okada Takahiko (b. 1939), and Yoshimasu Gōzō (b. 1939)—who emerged in the coterie magazines like *Drumcan* of the early 1960s, could immediately find their places side by side with the poets of the fifties when the poetry "boom" began after 1965.

Japan shares abundantly in the irony of the modern affluent society, where the works of radical poets who reject that society are well printed on good paper in substantial editions. Here there is a very great change from the Proletarian days of the 1930s when poetry was subject to police supervision and confiscation. Another very notable change is the appearance of so many women poets in post-war Japan. Yosano Akiko, at the beginning of the century, though not entirely without fellows, stands out in her remarkableness. A woman poet like Nagase Kiyoko was still very much an exception in the 1930s, but in the post-war period women have steadily increased their representation in poetry circles. No less than ten of the first sixty-five poets of the Shichōsha Library are women. Tomioka Taeko, Kōra Rumiko, and Ishigaki Rin are among the Mr H. prize-winners; Yoshihara

Sachiko and Shinkawa Kazue have won Murō Saisei prizes.

In the post-war period, too, especially in the last ten years, Japanese poets have begun to enter more widely into the international world of poetry. Before the Second World War, Japanese poets (or Japanese who were later to become poets) might, like others, go abroad to study, but few—Yone Noguchi (Noguchi Yonejirō, 1875–1947) and Horiguchi Daigaku are exceptions—made any significant contact with poets or even academics in Western countries. In large measure also the introduction of Western poetry and Western poetic theories, to which frequent reference has been made here, was carried out by Japanese themselves. Now Japanese poets are increasingly invited abroad, while British and American poets teach in or visit Japan. Although translation of Japanese literature into Western languages still falls far behind the translation of foreign literature into Japanese, it too has enjoyed a "boom" in the last ten years, and poetry has shared in the "boom". Much of this translation has been produced by the collaboration of Westerners and Japanese, although with the remarkable competence that more and more Japanese achieve in English and the increasingly international nature of the thought and expression of contemporary Japanese poetry, the merely linguistic aid that Japanese are likely to need may be very slight.

The road that the pioneers opened in 1882 has been steadily followed by their successors who have pursued a continuous quest for the modern. This, they have found in the poetry of the West and increasingly in company with poets of the West. But what of the *Japaneseness* of poems which now often translate rather readily into English and of which the content, though arresting, may impress the English reader with its novelty rather than with any sense of a foreign culture? The pioneers' aim in this regard may seem not always to have been so well fulfilled. Yet to judge this fairly we probably need to know much more of the context of the poems in the lives and attitudes of their writers. In the bringing of the lives and critical writings of these poets before Western readers almost everything still remains to be done.

Sydney   A.R. Davis

NOTES

1. Ochiai's poem was in fact a translation into Japanese of a Chinese poem by Inoue Tetsujirō. There is a German translation by Karl Florenz: *Weissaster*, published in Tokyo in 1895.
2. The absence of dates after a poet's name indicates that he is represented in this anthology and appears in the biographical notes.
3. It became independent of the New Japan Literary Society after August 1958 and was run for the remaining six years of its life by young poets who formed a Contemporary Poetry Society (Gendaishi no Kai). Sekine Hiroshi was editor with a committee which included Tanikawa Shuntarō and Ōoka Makoto.

SHIMAZAKI TŌSON
(1872–1943)

First Love

When you first combed back your fringe
Under the apple boughs
I thought you were like a flower
With the comb like a blossom at the front.

When you stretched out your white hand to me
To give me the apple
I felt for the first time the stir of love
Among the rose-red fruits of autumn.

I breathed my love like a sigh
Upon your combed-back fringe.
I gave you my heart
Like a cup brimming with the wine of love.

The path lies empty before me now
Under the tree in the apple orchard,
When I ask: "Who walked beside me along this narrow path?"
What I am missing is that first love.

Over the thousands of waves
   Ebbing and flowing
Upon the floating harp of the sea —
The waves all together in hundreds of ripplings
   Playing profound music —
And there comes a moment when
   We hear clearly from far away
The sound of the tides in spring.

Voyage over a Sea of Clouds

How refreshing the sounds of the oars
　　Beating upon the sea!
Clouds are floating over the immense sky
　　As my boat drives on, cleaving the waves.

Try to look into the depths of the blue deep —
　　Gazing through its still heaven
It is not possible for the eye to plumb its space
　　Where drifting leaves are rising, sinking.

It is not like a spring pulsing from under green grasses.
　　This is the tide of himself
That goes on flowing and flowing
　　Forever into the ocean's bed.

Distant white sails are flocks of sheep
　　In a meadow shepherded
By driving winds, and running
　　In the field of the sea.

A ship follows a cloud.
　　If the ship runs, the cloud
Chases it where sky and water meet —
　　The end of another day's voyaging.

TSUCHII BANSUI
(1871–1952)

Evening Star

The clouds are adrift and torn to rags
Around one star in the evening sky —
But though its radiance is shallow still
Its love is deep as ever in the sea of sky.

O, a shepherd in Chaldea
Saw you four thousand years ago —
And though your light is young for ever
Our world has now become so old.

Your sparkling light seems wet with dew —
Are you weeping for the men of earth?
Contentment in our world is far away,
Hidden by clouds of struggling anxiety and weariness.

YOSANO AKIKO
(1878–1942)

Never Let Them Kill You, Brother!

(Anxious thoughts about my brother Sōshichi with the besieging army
at Lüshun*)

Oh, brother, I am weeping for you.
Never let them kill you, brother!
You, the youngest son, the most beloved of our parents.
Did they teach you to kill others by the sword?
Did they bring you up to the age of twenty-four
Just in order that you could be killed killing others?

You, a shopkeeper, the young master and heir of an old and famous
Long-established confectionery store in Sakai, Osaka. So, brother,
Never let them kill you!
What does it matter whether Lüshun castle fall or not?
That kind of thing has nothing to do with us shopkeepers, has it?

Never let them kill you, brother!
The Emperor does not come out to fight.
How can his noble thoughts allow
That his subjects should fight bloody battles
And die like beasts, mistakenly believing
It is honourable to die?

Oh, brother, never let them kill you in battle!
Our poor mother, bereaved of father
Only last autumn, then deprived of her beloved son, is now
Rapidly growing grey — in this great reign
Which we are told is so secure.

How could you forget
Your lovely young bride, who is bitterly weeping for you
    behind the curtain,
A poor girl deprived of her husband
After no more than ten months' married happiness?
She loves and depends on no one but you. So, brother,
Never let them kill you!

* Called Port Arthur by the Russians and pronounced Ryojun in Japanese.

6   YOSANO AKIKO

You ask me to explain our love.
How can I explain it?
I shall compare it to a little tower
Whose foundation is our life
Whose central pillar is our love
Whose manifold storeys are learning and art
Bound with the mortar of our sweat and blood.

It shall be a tower of immense height.
We shall build it higher and higher
So that it may receive more wind and rain. But
Where we stand now is still quite lowly,
What we command here is still quite narrow,
We are without much sunshine here where it is
As cold as February. And
All we have to depend on is a small
Radiance burning within.

KITAHARA HAKUSHŪ
(1885–1942)

Unrequited Love

The acacia's leaves of red and gold are falling,
Falling in the dusky autumn light.
The heartache of my unrequited love
Shivers with cold along the river where the boats
Are beached. — Softly your sighs are falling on me,
Falling like the acacia's leaves of red and gold.

ISHIKAWA TAKUBOKU
(1885?–1912)

From *A Handful of Sand*

Songs of Self-love

1

White sand beach
On an island in
The eastern sea —
I toy with baby crabs
My face wet with tears.

14

Just for fun
I take Mother on my back
But she's so light
I wept and could not
Carry her more than three steps.

Smoke I

2

How can I
Relive that spring
Of my fourteenth year
When I softly spoke my own name
And melted into tears?

Fragments

1

Red! Red!
Thanks to the colour red
How very lively this world has become!

2

Flowers, women, flags,
And — blood!
The sinking sun of desert
Waves, signs of war adrift on oceans.

3

"O what sadness!"
Absent-mindedly
I happened to utter these words
In a passionate voice.
I was trying to awaken the memory of
One melancholy state of mind —
Yawn!

A little later, I thought, "Shall I kill myself?
There's nothing left for me but to kill myself."

4

What stillness!
There is not one echo
In the ravines at the back of my mind.

I strained my ears,
Thinking some sound must make itself heard,
And I spied the state of my mind until
The memory of that woman floated up.

"Yes, I'll go." I got ready to go at once.

"We'll meet and tell each other lies."

5

Do you want me to say something?
So you want me to laugh?
Yes, yes, I know —

Love masquerades as a coquette.
Sad woman!

Wait a second, just a second,
Only a fraction of a second —

For a moment, I found I could not laugh.
It's a bad habit I have.

The Horrors of a Summer Street

Under a scorching summer sun
The glaring rails —
Terror-stricken tracks of thought.

A tubby little three-year-old
Slides off his dozing mother's knee,
Toddles towards the tram-tracks.

At a greengrocer's, wizened vegetables.
Curtains at infirmary windows hang motionless.

Below the shut iron gates of a kindergarten
A white dog with long ears lies sprawling.

In the infinite brightness, somewhere,
Poppy petals flop down dead.

Melancholy of summer air — a live tree
Cracks open like a coffin.

An iceman's sickly wife comes out of her shop
Lugging a wooden workbox and holding up a broken-ribbed umbrella

In total silence,
Out of a boarding-house in a back street
A funeral procession
Crawls, into the horror of summer,
For the interment of a beri-beri victim.

A policeman at the corner gazes after it,
Stifling a yawn.

After a long-drawn-out stretch,
The white dog goes behind a rubbish bin.

Under a scorching summer sun
The glaring rails —
Terror-stricken tracks of thought.

A tubby little three-year-old
Slides off his dozing mother's knee,
Toddles towards the tram-tracks.

(First published 12 December 1909 in *Tōkyō Mainichi Shinbun*; republished with the following two poems and two others in the same newspaper under the collective title *Kokoro no Sugata no Kenkyū* [Studies of the Shapes of Feelings] in the following January)

Do Not Get Up

There is a life more shallow
Than this dusty window-pane
Warmed by the sinking sun.

A young man is taking an afternoon nap, snoring, sweating,
Dead tired with thinking.
Between his parted lips yellowish teeth.
Summer sun casts rays through the window-pane upon his hairy sh
And a flea is climbing up one leg.

Do not get up, do not get up until the sun goes down.
Until the cool, quiet evening sinks upon your life.

From somewhere comes a woman's coquettish laugh.

(First published 13 December 1909 in *Tōkyō Mainichi Shinbun*)

Fist

___

If I am pitied by a friend who's better off than me,
Or sneered at by a friend more powerful,
I lift my clenched fist in hot anger,
Only to discover at the back of my raging mind
A mind not raging, but
Huddled with nervously-blinking eyes
Like a wrongdoer nabbed red-handed —
What a helpless feeling!

O, the feeling of helplessness . . .

With this uselessly lifted fist
Whom
Shall I strike?

My friend? Myself?
Or that blameless wooden post over there?

(First published 20 December 1909 in *Tōkyō Mainichi Shinbun*)

I do not like the women of these parts.

What sadness, the wine accidentally spilt
Imperceptibly being absorbed
By the coarse paper of
This foreign book
With pages still unread.

I do not like the women of these parts.

15 June 1911, Tokyo

KINOSHITA MOKUTARŌ
(1885–1945)

Gold Dust Wine

EAU-DE-VIE DE DANTZIG
Wine with floating gold,
O maytime, maytime, liqueur goblet,
My bar's stained glass window
Purple in the rain falling on the city.

You woman, bar girl,
Already wearing summer silk
With narrow indigo stripes —
Pure white peony flower.
Don't touch. Your bloom would be scattered,
Your scent would be scattered.

O maytime, maytime, your voice is
The tune of a flute under the sweet paulownia blossoms,
The velvet fur of a young black cat,
The shamisen of our Japan, melting my heart.

EAU-DE-VIE DE DANTZIG
Because it is maytime, because it is May —

(at Americaya Bar)

MIKI ROFŪ
(1889–1964)

By the Swamp

A pale glimmer comes without a sound,
And dawn begins to spread across the snows.
A wind slightly stirs the branches of the trees
That stand like corpses intertwining empty arms.

It is then you appear beside the swamp,
A thin skin of ice upon its waters.
Darkness sways away like blown smoke.
How have you found your way to this place?
O, how could you take shape like this before my eyes?

Your face is melancholy as a sphinx,
Scarred by sorrows from beyond the grave.
Underneath the snows, what soul is burning?
Is that its harshly sobbing voice I hear?

Trees stand densely packed together like corpses.
A pallid daybreak now begins to move across the snows.
— Speak! Why do you stay silent by this desolate swamp?

TAKAMURA KŌTARŌ
(1883–1956)

Autumn Prayer

Autumn's austere vibrations fill the sky.
A sky of ultramarine blue, where birds are flying.

The soul neighs,
Pure water starts flowing in the heart.

The heart opens its eyes
And becomes a boy's again,
And all my convoluted past is laid before my eyes,
Still beating through all my veins.

Bathed in the autumn day, I remember more and more.
And give my blessing to activities within the earth
As I look back on my journey through life
With emotions close to tears.

I pray fervently,
But I can't find words to pray with —

Tears gathered
Fractured by sunlight.

I see falling leaves,
See animals running around joyfully,
See flying clouds and grasses blown by the wind in the garden —

Seeing the first cause's unremitting flow
My heart overflows with strong affection.

It also feels the endless responsibility unbearable.

I kneel down for joy, loneliness and terror,
But I can't find words to pray with —

I just pray by looking at the sky,
A sky of ultramarine blue.

Autumn's austere vibrations fill the sky.

Two at the Foot of a Mountain

Seen from the back, Bandai Mountain is split into
    two leaning parts.
That stare grimly at the August heavens overhead.
Horse-tail grasses wave in the wind, thick and wild,
Tall enough to hide a man, and flowing far away to
    the foot of the mountain.

My half-crazed wife is sitting on the soft green grass,
Leaning heavily against my arm
And wailing like a little girl, inconsolably crying:
— There will soon be no more hope for me —
Spirited away by the force of this demon of fatality,
Her mind is saying its inevitable farewell to the soul
In this irresistible foreboding:
— There will soon be no more hope for me —

The mountain wind's chill touch upon my hand wet with
    tears.
I gaze wordlessly at the spectacle of my wife's distress.
There is nothing in the world I can do now
To rescue this wife who clings to me as she turns
Finally away from the frontier of sanity.

And finally I feel my heart begin to break, splitting in two,
Becoming one absolutely with the universe that arches
    over us both.

Specimen

Snowing again today, a snow of idiot honesty,
Upon a numb, dumb cottage inside which
Is the specimen, a specimen of plain stupidity
From a certain country where he has existed
Through three periods of history,
Survivor disciplined by the whip of a peculiar
      moral code.
The rebellious pinions of a powerful eagle
Torn by the talons of terror he painfully polished
      himself
Have been prisoned for sixty years in a cage of iron law.
There he sits stiff and straight, giving all his heart
To this peculiar moral code he has lived for all
      his life,
This creature with his plain dumb honesty as idiotic
As the snow that never stops falling.

Now, released, he stretches his wings, to see
The sad reality of his present self —
The old feathers moulting and falling,
The eyes brightly flecked with dark green blind spots,
Yet breathing quietly still
Within the ruin of those four collapsing walls
Facing up to the vast stretches of nothingness before him —
This specimen of idiot honesty.

This is the specimen inside the mountain cottage
Which is slowly buried by the plain dumb honesty of snow,
The snow that is falling only as it must,
Foolishly falling endlessly even after it has covered all
      the world.

    TAKAMURA KŌTARŌ

YAMAMURA BOCHŌ
(1884–1924)

Dance

Storm
Storm
Irradiate the weeping willow
The bud
Of a baby's navel
The mercury's hysteria
I feel spring's arrival
Through the soles of my feet
Stop the storm
And let us make sad cups of oolong tea
In the samovar of love —
Kick the storm back up into the sky!

One Greenfinch is Chirping in That Treetop

Clear azure sky.
Way up high,
One greenfinch is chirping in that treetop.

Until yesterday, the tree,
Flexing its trunk like a spine,
Soughing in the gale —
One greenfinch is chirping in that treetop.

The tree is radiant with yesterday's wet:
The treetop leaves, refreshed, are glossy,
Shining in the morning light,
Swaying and spreading like smoke —
One greenfinch is chirping in that treetop,

Well, what of it? Some people may say
Such things do not put rice in our mouths
While others are toiling and suffering hardship.

All life on earth is suffering and hardship.
— But way up high, in true tranquility,
One greenfinch is chirping in that treetop.

Clouds

On the hilltop
Old man
Young child
Dreamily
Watching clouds.

HAGIWARA SAKUTARŌ
(1886–1942)

Tender Love

With your truly charming hard teeth,
Woman, you chew the green of the grass,
Woman,
With this pale green grass ink,
I will paint your face all over,
And arouse your passions;
Then let us play secretly together in the tall grass.
Look,
Here spotted bell-flowers are nodding their heads,
There gentians are moving their hands gracefully,
O I will clasp your breasts tightly,
You yourself will hug me in the strongest embrace.
Then in this empty field,
Let us play like snakes,
I myself will enfold you tightly tightly,
And wet your lovely skin with the sap of the green grass leaf.

Buddha

Or *"The Riddle of the World"*

In a hilly region of plentiful red clay
You sleep in a lonely cave
You are not a shell-fish nor a bone nor a thing
Nor do you seem an old rustic clock
Left lying on the sands where shore-weeds withered.
O are you the shadow or the ghost of "Truth"?
Mummy you have been sitting there for years and years
Living like a mysterious fish.
At this end of the unendurably desolate wasteland
The seas roar against the skies
And there sounds in the distance the surging approach
      of a tidal wave.
Can you hear it?
Eternal being Buddha!

MURŌ SAISEI
(1889–1962)

The Cicada Season

Somewhere or other
I can hear a cicada singing —
Shee-ee —
Can the cicada season be already here again?
   O where has he gone,
   My boy who went to hunt
   The first cicadas across the hot sands?
You poor, short-lived creatures of a summer,
In the distances of sky, the roofs of the town,
I hear the cicadas singing again —
Shee-ee —

Elephant

On an antique blue china dish
There is an elephant with a blue shadow
Being led along by a boy.

Because this dish is ancient
The bottom is uneven, the shadow of the elephant
Become dark indigo.
It seems to spread its lonely shadow
Even beyond the edges of the dish.

On such an antique blue dish
I see the solitary depths frozen like lacquer.
When evening comes,
The shadow of the elephant does not grow any longer,
But somehow shorter, and then it looks especially sad.

I love tense ice.
I love that intense emotion.
I saw it blazing like a rainbow.
I love that flower that is not a flower.
I feel deep sympathy with what it holds in its depths.
I share its sword-sharp passion.
Confined to the desert of my narrow existence
I am always pining. That is why
I love tense ice.
I know that intense emotion.

MUSHANOKŌJI SANEATSU
(1885–1976)

Pumpkins and Potatoes

The painter is now going to paint
three pumpkins and five potatoes.
He sees a variety of pumpkins:
a brown one, a green one, a yellow one,
a smooth one, a rugged one.
As they are so interesting a combination,
he is eager to find out the best arrangement for them.
Then in the foreground he places five potatoes
all of the same colour but of different shapes.
The painter, taking each pumpkin and potato one
     by one,
arranges them this way or that,
until he finally succeeds in giving each
the right position in the right place.
Now they are poised in harmony,
each looking its best, displaying its own distinct
     personality.
The painter takes up his brush
and with a contented smile on his face
says to himself: "This time I'll bring it off!"

SENKE MOTOMARO
(1888–1948)

Wild Geese

Across the warm, tranquil evening sky
A hundred or so wild geese flying in one long line.

They are curiously silent on the still
Backcloth of unmoving earth and sky.

Each one moving his wings in time with all the rest
Purposefully driving on in a single black line,
Without a sound across the evening sky.

If we were up there with them, the noise of their wings
Must be deafening, and some must be very weary,
Panting for breath.

But here on the ground we can know none of that
As they keep on flying, always encouraging one another,
Silently helping and caring for one another.

As they fly on, the front becomes the rear,
And the rear becomes the front, one heart beating for all,
Purposefully beating and flying ever onwards to their home.

There must be many parents and children among them,
There must be brothers and sisters and friends as well
All flying together through the soft, windless air

Like one body, – O, great warm heart beating in one body,
Soaring away through the stillness of sky and earth

Silently, with a miraculous swiftness,
Speeding away out of sight as I stand watching their flight.

Secret

When it is time for the little boy to go to bed
He runs naked and laughing through the house
Like a bird escaped from its cage
Or a prince sprung out of a magic box.
He runs stamping his bare feet round the house,
Bumping his head, banging his hands or his bottom
On anything that stands in his way — on the sliding doors
Of paper, on the walls — rejoicing in the feel of the cool air.

His mother is chasing after him with his little pyjamas.
A little boy naked is skinny as a water-sprite —
He is driven into a corner at last, and
Waits there breathlessly, pressing himself against the wall,
So very tiny he looks, with his face to the wall.
Then his mother catches him and quickly covers him up
As if they shared a secret no one else must know.

Fallen Leaves

As I was wandering along a mountain path
I found a number of freshly fallen yellow leaves
Of a giant magnolia tree, scattered along the way,
Resembling, with their bent-back tips, Chinese slippers.
O! the sudden revelation of this brilliant colour
Made me feel as if certain noble persons
Had just taken off their shoes and left them there,
Then departed on bare feet,
Leaving this quietness
That turns the path into the landscape of a dream.

SATŌ HARUO
(1892–1964)

Song of the Mackerel Pike

O! Autumn winds,
If you have any pity at all,
Go and tell her for his sake —
That a man is sitting here
Alone at his supper table
Eating broiled pike,
And lost in thoughts of his wife gone away.

Mackerel pike,
Over which the man
(After the fashion of his folk at home)
Squeezes the sour juice of a green tangerine
And eats the fish —
Curious, then endearing
This rustic habit in the man —
She used always to bring for his supper
Such a freshly picked green tangerine . . .

A pitiful sight —
The wife who is to be forsaken by her husband
And the husband betrayed by his wife
Sit facing each other across the supper table;
While a little girl, unloved by her father,
Is struggling, sadness in her heart,
With her own tiny chopsticks,
Trying to offer this man who is not her father
A bit of her own fish.

O! Autumn winds,
Behold this homely gathering,
A sight out of this world —
Autumn winds,
Prove that this
Happy gathering is not just a dream.

O! Autumn winds,
If you have any heart,
Go and say to
The wife whose husband has not yet deserted her
And the little girl whose father has not yet gone away
That a man is sitting here
Alone at his supper table
Eating broiled pike,
And letting fall salty tears.

O! Mackerel pike,
Are you salt or bitter?
In what land is it the custom
To eat mackerel pike
With hot tears squeezed over it?
O! Is the question I am asking quite absurd?

(This poem was first published in the magazine *Ningen* [Mankind]
in 1921. Its reference is to Satō's love for Chiyo, the first wife of his
friend the novelist Tanizaki Jun'ichiro [1886–1965]. After a period of
estrangement between the two writers from 1921 to 1927, Tanizaki
divorced Chiyo so that Satō might marry her in 1930.)

The young man was born of the sea.
Nourished on the breasts of the swelling sails.
Grew up magnificently big.
One day he went out to sea
And returned no more.
Perhaps with that grave gait of his he
Moved with long strides out into the sea.
The bereaved
Wept and erected a small tombstone.

HORIGUCHI DAIGAKU
(b.1892)

The Time of Eventide Is a Good Time

The time of eventide is a good time,
A time exceedingly tender.

It does not matter what the season is —
In winter by a fireside,
In summer in the shade of big trees —
It is always full of mystery,
It is always a time that charms people's hearts,
Murmuring softly, as if it knew that people's hearts
Love to seek, now and then, silence and stillness . . . . .

The time of eventide is a good time,
A time exceedingly tender.

For those still young and happy
It is a time full of fondlings and caresses,
It is a time overflowing with tenderness,
It is a time full of hope.
For lost people far from the dreams of their youth
It is a time of tender memory,
A time of intoxication with dreams long past.
It is a pain that wounds them to the heart,
Though they never forget the lingering fragrance of days gone by.

The time of eventide is a good time,
A time exceedingly tender.

Where does this melancholy of the eventide come from?
Nobody knows!
(O, and does anybody know about anything?)
Yet with the approach of night it grips us closer,
Leading us further into deeper fantasy . . . .

The time of eventide is a good time,
A time exceedingly tender.

The time of eventide —
All nature then seems to offer us repose —
Winds drop,
Sounds die away,
We can hear the breathings of flowers,
Blades of grass blown by the wind are deathly still,
Birds bury their heads beneath their wings . . . .

The time of eventide is a good time,
A time exceedingly tender.

Sea Scene

A seagull practises pothooks
On the slate of the sky.

The sea is a grey meadow
With white waves like flocks of sheep.

A steamer is going for a stroll
Puffing away at a pipe.

A steamer is going for a stroll
And giving a whistle from time to time.

Poetry

I want to seek my poetry in pain and hardship.
I want to write a poem irrevocable once written.

A house without beams or pillars
But that stays firmly upright,

Each line supporting the other, each word
Echoing through its neighbour.

I want a poem that never comes to an end at its end.
I want to find my poetry in pain and hardship.

OZAKI KIHACHI
(1892–1974)

Young Silver Birch

Drenched in the green airs of morning
The slender branches lash like whips;
Though the young leaves are tender with rising sap
They are not yet thick enough to hide
The birds singing complaints of love.

Drunk with the springtime's exhalations,
It simply stands there, reaching up tall and silvery
Out of enchanted drifts of primrose, lily-of-the-valley,
Till it touches the stern mountain peak glittering with snow.

Autumn River Landscape

to my daughter Eiko

Two days' rain has cleared up without trace.
This morning, a new wind is blowing between sky and earth.
Look at that small stone on the sun-warmed ground —
It is called diorite.
Even such small stones all bear their own fine names.
Each and every one is warmed by sun, blown by wind.
In today's fresh weather, like a day from times gone by;
Like a dream of something tender in the memory,
Everything is casting a cool, pale-blue shadow.

A river comes into sight among the vineyards.
Never forget this heartfelt joy we feel
When natural waters appear in a landscape!
On both banks of the river, running like tangled silver threads,
On the plain, on the hills, and everywhere
The native folk's hopeful life goes on,
In the cultivated fields spread out before us like a picture.
Over this beautiful and spacious river landscape
There extends the same sky as in Japan in autumn,
And over the many different ways of life that go on over there .

TANAKA FUYUJI
(b.1894)

Homage to the *Daikon*

Daikon like the horned moon
Though it is still-life, cold,
If you slice it snickety-snack
The cut part is full of juice
And its fresh smell sprays all over.

O holy cross-shaped flower
The diffused radiance of the fields
Is heavy with you.

This particular vegetable
has indeed a mind of its own
in its splendid self-sacrifice
wearing its halo with joy.

The *daikon* is also
Much sounder than our sick human thoughts,
Setting foot upon our earth
With the bright, lively steps of angels.

Daikon: a root vegetable, commonly called the Japanese radish; it is
white, smooth-skinned, and shaped like a very large parsnip.

NISHIWAKI JUNZABURŌ
(b.1894)

Mutability

I am this pathetic scrap of history leaning on the handrail of
    the balcony,
Gazing at the slopes of Meguro radiant with narcissi,
A landslip of red clay grown with clumps of bamboo grass —
I gaze upon these from this pure white leaning tower.
The setting sun lies like a wet lotus blossom on the swimming
    pool
Whose garden lawn is dry and withered.

In this atelier-like salon hung with gamboge curtains
The host, a collector of antique Western glasses and goblets
Was explaining about lead, enamel, and crystal
To the wise men from the East.

Then at the banquet the wise men were talking together
And leaning over the ladies on either hand as if they were lovers.

Nora poured the wine elegantly.
(Whenever there is a sprinkle of snow on bamboo grass,
And I hear the cry of the pheasant, I remember this lost night.)

Soon I was feeling light-headed,
Caught in the painful embrace of the goddess.
If I keep still I feel sick.
I curse wine.
I pace up and down like a tiger.
Then I seemed to get a glimpse of a book of ancient songs
But it was *Verres Anciennes*, not *Vers Anciens*.

Most of the guests had gone.
I feel the mutability of life
As I dance with the evening's destiny hanging over me,
Dancing limply with a woman straight as an iris,
An infinity of woman,
A woman like a May breeze
With this woman delicate as Euphrosyne.
I dance with this infinite woman,
While the tears of loneliness wet my cheeks.

At the beginning of September, we two men walked together.
Fluent with philosophy, the words flowed out of us.
And there was nothing left for us to think about.

Memory with us was merely biological, especially the flora.
Mosses and lichens could be left to the care of temples.
We were secretly pleased to discover that mushrooms and bindweeds
Already expressed humanity in finished symbols.

This male friend of mine was wearing a crepe shirt
With a pattern of butterflies. It was more or less
Desirable, looking rather like a tea-gown worn by
Some secret mistress in black high-heeled shoes.

We asked a girl who came our way on a bicycle
About the whereabouts of the Ekoma Waterworks.
We did not divulge thoughts of the young bucks who used to
Show their refinement using the clean waters of the Tamagawa,
As the courtesans of old Edo used to say.

There were balsams blooming in the garden of a farmhouse
Reminding us of childhood, and we whispered:
"Who does not know the balsam flower?" At the same time
Deploring the fact that our balsam civilization
Was going to rack and ruin.

I said: "I wish Rakuō had built himself a retreat here,
Instead of banishing himself deep in the country.
Then he might have created something even better than
The Katsura Detached Palace. What a pity!"

Seeing a house of substance surrounded by zelkova trees and
A bamboo thicket, apparently an ancient dwelling owned by
A former landed proprietor, we sniffed the air, sensing
A certain something about it.

Plucking from an age-old tree some red berries and leaves,
I put them under my friend's nose, saying:
"This is Japanese pepper. An old wheelwright
Once hanged himself here on this tree."

Though there was a milestone saying "This way to Edo-Aoyama,"
We still managed to lose our way. Anyhow
We thought we'd better get back to the station, and on the way
Asked directions of the young wife of a greengrocer, who claimed
She was once a dancer at the "Casablanca", and then
We made our way towards the Keigan-ji Temple.

As night was coming on, we started trotting like wild things.
The concrete road had bend after bend as it ran beside
The river dense with thickets of yellow-eared sumac bushes.

We had been hunting for "some big September story".
Around eight, we ate bowls of buckwheat noodles in Shinjuku,
And when we got back to Meguro we visited
An antique dealer like a woman by Renoir,
And over cups of green tea we talked about
How many forged paintings there were bearing Kōkan's signature —
And then we went our different ways.

KANEKO MITSUHARU
(1895–1975)

Gold Bug

When the silhouettes of willow-trees are dark with mourning
    wreaths of smoke,
When the yellow flowers of the clove are dropping gently to
    the ground,
When the new moon is rising like a silver wire —
A lovesick boy is moaning
As a gold bug yearns all night for the lighted lamp.

This night, the boy is holding in his arms the sacred image of
A girl as beautiful as almond-blossom,
The boy's burning cheeks are glowing like peaches.
His bashful panting makes him flush like crimson shellfish.

In fear and trembling at the thought of touching her,
The boy's heart, sad but true, was swarming with anxiety,
Like a shoal of little minnows.

The boy was filled with confusions and disturbances,
Swayed like a scarlet seaweed in the boughs of lust and loss.

The boy was devastated, body and soul, like a shattered wreck.
Ah — drugged with the fumes and fragrances of aloes,
The boy became a figure of fun.
    (The taste of first love should be delicate!
    Sweet is the flight into hells of love!)

Seal

I

How foetid the breath
Steaming from his mouth —
His back wet and clammy like the edge of a grave-hole.
It all makes us feel sick with black despair.
O, what misery . . .

Its body's dead weight and languor, like a sandbag,
Gloomily elastic — glum rubber —
Self-admiring — banality incarnate —

Pockmarks —
Big balls —

"I was always trying to get away from the rest
As I was shoved around by crowds that
Made my nose blue with their stink.
The jostling town they are racing through like swarming clouds
Was for me as lonely as Alaska in a scratchy old movie."

II

These — these vulgar crowds, as they are called —
These are the masses that drove Voltaire into exile
And thrust Hugo Grotius into prison.

From Batavia to Lisbon
These are the ones who dominate the dust and blather of the worl

Seal sneezing — seal spitting decayed shreds of fish
From yellowed teeth, from bristling whiskers —
Suppressing yawns — affected gestures —
These are the ones who congregate screaming
Traitor — you madman —
Pointing their fingers at breakers of convention.
They all seem to be each other's wives and husbands,
Each other's lovers and mistresses too.
Their sons take after them — even to the ill nature —
Dirty cyclings of blood.

Sometimes they form cliques
And these cliques link with other cliques
And their endless cliques and links create a wall of bodies
That seems to dam the tides.
Sunlight shot with sleet pouring over the withdrawing waves.
And always the wire nets imprisoning infinities of sky.

Today a wedding.
Yesterday a holiday — but all day long
In the slush they heard the ice-breaker
Breaking up the ice.

Bowing to each other all the time, rubbing themselves with fins
Rolling their bodies like barrels,
Hustling and bustling meaninglessly, grubbily,
Wallowing in dirty sea-water foaming with their own piss,
Keeping each other warm by body contact,
Hating the cold, abandoning disintegrating groups,
They call to each other in feeble voices,
Longing for the sympathy of other eyes.

III

O they — not one of them noticed that
The iceberg they are living on, darker than a midnight town,
Was starting to disintegrate and slide away into the abyss.

They go stumbling over the ice on fan-shaped, useless tails
Talking about literature and so on . . .

The sad evening shades into a hanging scroll
Where the sun declines like a great swollen chilblain!

Dragging their long shadows like zebra stripes on the snow,
The masses bow their heads all together in worship,
Bowing their heads as one, as far as the eye can reach.

But with an air of open contempt,
One alone
Is facing composedly in the opposite direction.

I am that one.
I am that seal who, disliking my fellow seals,
Can still be nothing but a seal among seals.

All I can do is
To turn my back on what the others bow to.

A Song for Bubbles

I

Where have all the bubbles gone?

Light and frail, and on the point of
shattering at the merest touch.

Where have they gone,
those happy-go-lucky dreams?

Where have they been spirited to,
those sweet dances and singings?

Rosy bubbles,
rosy sweat on the skin of roses.
No sooner blooming
than bidding farewell to us,
flying away into the sky,
a momentary attraction.

Travelling rainbows.

The bubbles we
pursue
at the heart of devastation.

Big bubbles, little bubbles,
where have they all gone?

Were they beauties that had to perish
just to be born immortal in my heart?

Celestial nymphs shimmering on air,
more fragrant than irridescent crystal.

II

They say an Emperor of China in days gone by
followed you up to the peak of Kunlun-shan.
O you bubbles,
paeans to a past that is no more.

Ascension of trends.

A company of mimes
dwindling upwards, upwards.

A bevy of schoolgirls.

A lustre on cheeks that are no more.
Evaporated poems.

All those I've lost sight of
since around 1940.

Those who were scattered by gunfire,
those who ran away from the clutches of politics.

Where are you flying
                    now?

Where in the heavens
are you drifting?

Dear bubbles!
Dear bubbles!

Sailors with bad memories say they saw you
off the coast of Africa
Explorers, big mouths, declare modestly, as if
they had witnessed it with their own eyes, that seals
were balancing you on their noses in the ice of northern waters.

MIYAZAWA KENJI
(1896–1933)

The Morning I Said Farewell to My Sister

O my sister,
You who before the day is over will be going far away from here,
It's sleeting outside and it all seems strangely bright
    (Brother will you bring me some snow).
From very gloomy clouds of dull red
Snow is wetly falling mixed with rain
    (Brother will you bring me some snow).

I jump up and rush like a crooked bullet into the dark sleet
Carrying two cracked bowls with patterns of vegetable leaves
To get some snow for you.
    (Brother will you bring me some snow.)
From sombre clouds the colour of pale lead
The sleet is wetly dropping in the slush.

O, Toshiko, sister,
You've asked me to bring you a simple bowl of snow
Just when you are dying, to brighten the rest of my life —
Thank you, my brave sister!
From now on, Toshiko, my life shall be clean and straight!
    (Brother will you bring me some snow.)
Panting with harsh, harsh fever, you asked me
For a last bowl of snow from the sky,
From the world above that is known as the galaxies,
The kingdoms of the sun, and outer space . . .

Upon two blocks of granite
Wet slush is piled in chill loneliness.
I stand unsteadily on them
To gather from the gleaming pine branch
Handfuls of crystal cold drops
Of icy water still milky with snow —
Gather them for my sweet sister, her final food
Today you will be parting from even these
Familiar blue-patterned bowls
That we have known since we were children.
    (Brother, this is a journey I can only take alone.)

Yes, surely you are leaving us today,
O my brave sister lying in the shuttered sickroom
Behind the dark folding screen
Or within the pale mosquito-net
You burn away your life, so white and weak,
O my brave sister.

The snowlight is all around us —
This radiant snow descended from
That frightening, turbulent sky.
    (When I am born again, if I have human form,
    I shall not live to suffer only for myself.)

O my sister, I pray that theses two bowls of snow
Will be transformed for you into the food of heaven —
I pray so from the bottom of my heart —
And pray that some day they may be turned for everyone
Into a holy manna here on earth.

Farewell

Perhaps you couldn't realize what harmonies your bass was making
So much simplicity hope and joy set me almost trembling like blade
    of grass.
If you are to comprehend all the characteristics of those sounds
And their fine and infinite permutations so clearly
As to be able to command them freely at any time you choose, then
You will be embarked upon a difficult but brilliant calling.

At an early age all famed European musicians
Made themselves masters of violin or piano, as you
Of our native instruments, shoulder-drum or bamboo flute.
Now I suppose we have at least five out of all the tens of thousands
Who are young like you in our nearby towns and villages
And who could be compared with you for genius and talent.
Yet I fear that every one of them, in another five years or so,
Will dissipate their genius and their talent.
For some, the struggle for existence will blunt their skills.
Others will lose them before they know it, out of idleness.
Neither genius nor talent nor resourcefulness can last for ever.
(No man will stay with you for ever, either.)

I haven't told you yet, but I am leaving this school
Before the new term begins. Perhaps we both
Will have to follow a dark, steep path through life. But
I hope and pray your youth may never be tarnished,
That you never lose those lovely sounds
Of true harmony and radiant light —
That you never lose them irretrievably, for then
I should never want to see you again.
I hate nothing more than the great majority
Who rest effortlessly upon their mediocre talents.

Please remember what I am telling you, my dear:
In days to come, if you think lovingly of some young girl,
You will see before you infinite images of light and shade.
Never fail, then, to blend them into harmony, despite
All the loneliness you feel as you labour cutting weeds
In solitude, in a stony wilderness, while the others
Waste their time in towns or laze their days away.

Sing under the burdens of insult and poverty!
And if you find no instrument to play on, you, my pupil
Must play with all your being on
That sky-filling pipe organ made of radiant illuminations!

MARUYAMA KAORU
(1899–1974)

Spirit of the Water

Even when the water is clear   his spirit is deeply troubled
Shivering with apprehension
The water wants to keep peace with himself
But sometimes he has to raise his voice

The water is whipped by the will   but he can smell things   and
      breathe
For he has feelings he can not control

His emotions are shattered   become confused   lose hope
He suddenly tilts   stands on his head —
Screams   crashes into smithereens —
Sometimes he wakes up from that kind of dream

After that his colour begins to fade
The water frequently prays he may regain his spirits
But such prayers are not easily answered

The water's heart overflows with longing to express itself
It really tries to speak of many things
But the words have no body

He often wonders where he first gushed forth
He feels mortified because he has no shape
Soon anger is building up   spreading   bursting its dams
And he can't bear it

He falls into a despair
But even in his sadness hoping to forget his face a moment
— For a moment he thought he'd forgotten it

The water has not yet opened his eyes
The sun is stroking the water's eyelids tenderly

Spring in the North

O what a wonder
This sudden noise of the dale
Gathering to itself the snows of the mountains —
Overflowing into the valley and plunging roaring on —
This terrifying thunder of water!

Released from the bonds of snow slowly loosening,
One by one, tree branches spring back into place:
They are jewelled with new, round little buds,
And could slash open a man's forehead with their bold whip.

The forest at the mountain's foot
Will soon put on a thin veil of green,
In which the white flowers of the wild magnolia
Will hasten to unfold.

Early morning. First class begins.
One of the girls put up her hand:
"Please, teacher, I saw
The first swallow!"

The Crested Crane

With that tilted, faded *chapeau* on her head,
She looks like a chic working girl.

Inside the wire cage, and many times a day
She flaps her wings — but only rarely
Raises in the air backward-flowing shanks,
And momentarily describes, so gracefully,
A rainbow arc above the fountain.

A few seconds, and her flight is over.
But that moment's dream release is longer
Than the free flight of crows and kites
In their ordinary sky.

For she
Never wakes up from her dream.

A Woman Called Sea

If asked how much I love you, I should say
I love you with all the fullness of your rising breast,
or as intensely as the tempest in your breast that rocks
even hundred-thousand-ton tankers.

But if asked why I love you, I could hardly find
a suitable answer.
As I stand there alone confusedly muttering,
you suddenly become swirling clouds of sea-birds or
a colossal rainbow of flying fish,
and make the earth a giant bait
to catch Uranus or Neptune.

O the thought of the world without you
is more dreary than death itself.
O my beloved old wife
still singing youthful songs,
you, a woman called sea.

MIYOSHI TATSUJI
(1900–1964)

Perambulator

Mother—
There is something falling, faint and sad.
There is something falling, the colour of hydrangeas.
In the shade of this endless avenue of trees
the wind blows murmuring.

It is evening.
Mother, push my pram.
Facing the setting sun with tears in its eyes,
push my pram with a tinkling sound.
Put on my head that feels the cold
a velvet cap with a red tassel.
You can see the season crossing the sky
in the lines of birds hastening away.

There is something falling, faint and sad—
here on the road where something is falling, the colour of hydrangea
Mother, I know, I know
this road leads far, far away.

On the Pavement

Lovely flowers are floating,
floating down on the young ladies.
The young ladies walk, talking softly to one another.
Footfalls, calmly, radiantly, float in the air.
From time to time, raising their eyes,
they pass the unshadowed temple of eternal spring.
The tiles of the temple roof are wet with mossy green
and under the eaves here and there
hanging bells have a quiet look.
And all alone
I make my own shadow walk the pavement.

Young Boy

At evening,
out of the gate of a certain monastery
comes a handsome young boy, going home.

At the end of a day quickly darkening
he throws up a hand-ball,
he throws a hand-ball high up in the sky
and continues playing on his way home.

In the quiet street
both man and trees look drained of colour,
and the sky goes flowing like a dream.

Village

The deer was put in a dark storeroom. His antlers were bound with
hemp ropes. Where nothing more could be seen, his blue eyes shone
clear and he sat upright with an elegant air. A potato was lying there.

Outside the cherry blossoms were falling, and down the
mountainside, a bicycle came rolling, printing a trail of flowers.
A girl was looking at the bamboo bush with her back toward us.
A black ribbon was pinned on the shoulder of her kimono jacket.

Spring

Goose: There are so many of us here together. I honk in order
         not to lose myself.
Lizard: I tried climbing every stone, and still my belly is cold.

Breakfast beside a Pond

The water is clear.
A drizzling rain is falling lightly and noiselessly.
The singing birds
change their accents every day.
I must call this lonely life a lonely life.
How many times did I stop eating breakfast
with chopsticks poised in my hand
and gaze at the glimmer of fish?
Then I sense, in a still undefined shape, the sorrow of the day.
Try to think of something pleasant.
With this in mind, I snatch at a vain hope,
yet the small fish, disappear in the water
and leave me familiar only with sorrow.

*Enfance finie**

An island far out in the sea . . . . A camelia dropped in the rain.
    Spring is in the bird cage.
  Spring in the bird cage containing no bird.

    All promises were broken.

    Clouds are reflected in the sea, and the earth in the clouds.

    There are staircases in the sky.

Today, the flag of memory was hauled down, and I will depart
    from people like a big river.
  There are my footprints on the floor, and on the footprints,
    specks of dust . . . . Ah, poor me,

    Now, am I not departing on a long journey?

Title in French

Crow

An overhead bamboo water-pipe crosses the road of a quiet village.
A crow is perching on it and in the sunbeams piercing the leaves
    of the trees
he looks up at the sky and looks down at the earth. When I
    passed below
he was swinging like a scale-pan with his wings at rest in delicate
    equilibrium.

Quiet Night

The tick-tock of the clock. Ah, the swallows of Time
are crossing the mountain, crossing the sea. What stillness!
In the woods, the owls are tapping a hand-drum. Finally these
    last few days
I have been able to face the night, looking at the wall, looking a

Stone-beating Birds

The leaves are turning yellow and day by day the mountains grow
    paler,
The river in the valley also thrusts away its green.
Two pairs of wagtails, one white, one yellow, say to me,
"The pebbles in this river are all rounded
because we have been beating them with our tails."

Losing a Friend [1]

Departure

The airship moved out of the hangar at midnight,
coughed hard for a while and spat up a rose of blood.
Dear Kajii—you went to heaven then and there.
My friend, this is only a brief separation . . . very soon I myself
    will come and see you!

Visting the Tomb

Dear Kajii—in the garden of the hospital that I am looking at
    from my window now
there are a goat and a kid crying together. Above the fresh
    green treetops, the clouds fly past.
Beyond the trees, the larks in the cage are singing.
It occurred to me that I should visit your tomb when I am out of
    hospital.

On the Road

With a music score rolled up in your hand, you came down the
    hill singing.
I was returning from the village swinging my stick.
. . . . A few clouds were visible in the sunset glow above the wheat
    fields.
That instant at once became fixed in my memory: Mt. Fuji
    appeared in the distance.

1. Kajii Motojirō (1901–35) was a fellow student of Miyoshi at the
Third Higher School in Kyoto. He had published a number of works
of autobiographical fiction in a poetic, melancholic vein before his
death from tuberculosis. Miyoshi was himself at this time in hospital.

Morning

Crows pass cawing. Now it is noon on a spring day.
My mind in mourning leans against the window. My friend.
My friend. The voice of the crows lost in the sky. The girls walking
    among the trees,
with their black hair shining in the sun. How sad, how beautiful! Ah,
    this instant of life lodged in my eyes!

Break of Day

Two or four pumpkin flowers blooming on the sand.
After forgetting to put out these lamps, where did the night go?
Across the river
Night had become a freight train, disappearing down a tunnel.

Frail Flowers

Frail flowers
Fragile flowers
Their life is fleeting.
Morning glories blooming at dawn
wither during the day.
Bindweed blooming during the day
withers in the evening.
Bottle-gourds blooming in the evening
wither in the morning.
All have a brief life.
But they are punctual.
They return on time.
They return I know not where.

I desire that several pear trees be planted
beside my tomb.

In spring their white flowers will be in bloom.
In autumn their sweet fruit will ripen.

Do not ask after the sad life
of the person asleep in the shade.

I do not know when it was
I learned my whole way of life from these trees.

Do not mock me for having no reason
to speak to people even about this.

How can I trust in anything,
even if I pour out feeling from the depths of my heart?

As the form of songs is like floating clouds
its traces soon vanish.

However, after time has passed
and the trees beside the tomb cast shade,
people will tie their horses to the trees
and travellers will rest there.

Meditating on those who are to come,
my heart is quite easy.

I desire that several pear trees be planted
beside my tomb.

Flag

Therefore, look at the flag flying from the top of the spire
of that dreamlike white architecture above the innumerable
windows floating far in the sky.
At the upper end of the flagstaff rising straight, higher and
thinner,
look, up there, too, I see a sea.
I see a flag flapping like a sea.
Indeed, countless waves rise one after another where air
currents flow,
surging endlessly from the deep, following each other slowly,
surging again today from the neighbouring mountain ranges,
from the bottom of the sky.
Numberless creatures pursue dreams soaring up to heaven:
A flock of pathetically gentle geese, goats, kids, sheep, milch
cows with calves.
Where are they hurrying to? Their shoulders heave and jostle
one another.
At a spot like this in heaven (— some are crying) their hopes
are extinguished one after another,
within that gloomy fenced space, in that slaughterhouse where
pigs unnumbered die.
Does it not look like this?
Over there in the sky that today has completely cleared, scale-
like clouds stand still, cold and frozen.
At the top of the spire of the white building towering as if in
a dream, there softly flies a flag hoisted so high that it
looks very tiny.
Ah! we always see such a flag, historical, flying above a city
where people dwell.

KITAGAWA FUYUHIKO
(b.1900)

Execution

Putrefying blast
The clumps of summer grass are blowing in the wind
Just like a human hair.
Out of this clump
A horse's neck and head are sticking.

At the end of the head on a neck stretching and shaking
This horse has a wide-open mouth
And it is foaming at the mouth —

He is panting
He is collapsing
(The surrounding gloom is caused by
This desperate panting).

The clump of summer grass
Is only just swaying,
Smoothly as if stroked by a hand stroking
The horse's muzzle —

The horse's mouth
Is open for no reason whatsoever —
He is pawing at nothing.

The horse's neck is stretched right out
And he keeps his foaming jaws wide open
The neck does not move at all now,
As if it had been hanged already —

Ah, but it is hanging without any rope —
Without any rope?

No, it is simply that we cannot see
With these eyes of ours
This most brutal execution —
This most uncalled-for execution.

Where has the rest of the body gone?
I can't see even one hind leg!

TAKAHASHI SHINKICHI
(b.1901)

No Meaning

Words are the last things we need.
We were better off without language in our lives.
We cannot find any better words to add to the first.
Yet those who know nothing of words are using them,
Giving them meanings of their own making.

Is there any meaning, after all, in a gun?
There is no meaning in killing our fellow men.
You may say it is a fact of life, but
Just because it is a fact does not invest it with meaning.
A fact is what actually exists, like
That blue flame on the charcoal before my eyes.
A fact means it existed, but no more.
Is there any meaning in what is no more?
There seems to be no greater nonsense
Than to concern oneself with things that are no more.

What does a horse live for?
Is there any meaning in her bearing a colt?
You may say that it is all a matter of relativity,
That everything is an accident.
You would be right.
And that is why you cannot express it in words.
There is nothing relative between what you express
And what you call a fact.
It is nothing but an accident; everything is an accident.
It is just as absurd to give a fact meaning as to give a word
        meaning.

What meaning is there in the fact that night continues dark?
What meaning in the fact that people die?
What meaning in the fact that snow falls?
What meaning in the fact that flowers are beautiful?
What meaning in my saying these things?
Yet they are all facts.

What on earth can be otherwise than facts? Everything is
A fact. And that is why everything has no meaning.
No meaning in cocks' crowing.
No meaning in the setting of eggs.
No meaning in flying in a plane.
No meaning in listening to the radio.
No meaning in reforming the government.
The dead have no meaning here.

Do the living have any meaning here?
No, every fact has no meaning.

Living, too, has no meaning.
You may say it is of some interest, but it is of no meaning.
It may be a fact. But
Every fact has no meaning.

83   TAKAHASHI SHINKICHI

My Body

I have been broken into pieces:
those green leaves thick on the persimmon tree
are my hands and feet rustling in the wind.

That bright-coloured butterfly fluttering by
has my eyes in those spots on her wings.

The future is surrounded by
a moving wall of earth.

A dog is pregnant with the earth,
the gods sucking its pointed nipples.

Each nipple is as big as the point on a red pencil.

I have been swimming in fire and water.
A plane has flown between my straddled legs.
The sky is my body.

Afterimages

The volcanic vapours of Mount Aso
Drifting on a sandbank across the sea.
Volcanic ash piled on the farm's mulberry leaves
And even snowing the heads of sparrows.

A crocodile of lava lies with ever-open jaws.
A sparrow alights upon a fossil-like branch,
Moonlight shining under its lids.
A monitor lizard immobilized on a decaying log,
Its tail quivering like a peninsula.

Clouds drifting through my head —
O, such beautiful clouds!
But when the sparrow opens its eyes
Everything vanishes — the sparrow
Is blind, though its eyes are open always,
Gazing at nothing but rose-lit space.

Don't say a red flower came into bloom there,
On that tree — all that moved was
The tip of a girl's nose, in close-up.
Everything now is no more than afterimages.

The intense coolness of water flowing underfoot,
The sparrow immured in the vertical pit of an urn,
Staring at the crater with half-open eyes, its wings
Fanning the fiery pillar that burns the earth to ashes.

HINO SOJO
(1901–56)

At the Miyako Hotel

Arriving to spend the night
With my wife wed today
The spring evening

The spring midnight
I am with my wife who's
Still a virgin

Close to our pillows
The light of spring burning
My wife puts it out

Can a woman
Be a thing like this
The spring darkness

Scent of roses
Our first night is turning
Grey

On my wife's forehead
Comes quick spring's
Morning glory

In the bright morning
Before the toast on our table
We feel shy

Just after the bath
Her face without make-up looks private
The spring afternoon

A long day
Our hands stay touching
When they brush

We remember
What we have lost—the pearly sky
Of cherry-blossom time

MURANO SHIRŌ
(1901–75)

Hammer Throw

Look!
In a world circumscribed by iron
A poor dynamo is panting momentarily

Set in a white circle.

Horizontal Bar

I

I know wretched octopuses
Drying on racks by the beach.

I too was strung in the air,
The hypothetical bar supported me.

My thoughts slid down
And ran out of my nose.
I hiccupped,
Kicked the landscape aside
And dared to commit sacrilege in the sky.

Then, the bar
Swung me on to a new world.

For the first time I look down
Upon the startled faces
And treetops now ridiculously low.

II

I jump on the horizon's hoop —
Fingertips get a precarious grip on it.

Hung from another world,
My muscles are my last resort.
I turn red, contract,
My feet keep going up —
O, where am I off to?

89   MURANO SHIRŌ

The world comes full circle, all-enveloping,
And finds me high above —
With this wide view from above,
And O, the clouds draping my shoulders!

Pole Vault

Like a wasp
He comes dashing with a long pole
And floats up into the air
As if there were nothing to it,
Zooming up the rising horizon,
Until at last having jumped over the bar
He abandons what supported him,
Left stuck in earth.
Fall is now all that is left to him,
Oh, he is falling awkwardly —
Making a bad fall on his back flat on the ground
The horizon suddenly came down
Giving him a violent thump across the shoulders.

Dive

Clouds' raiment blooms like flowers,
Reflections on the water
Zebra-stripe your naked body.

Finally you leap outwards
With wings of muscles —
A small bee tanned by the sun.

You are falling now towards the flowers
And enter the water
Like a sudden sting.

After a while, from the shade of
The flowers over there, you surface.
Wet with so much water
You look unbelievably heavy now.

Like two hands which
Rising out of wide sleeves
Are joined high, the two bodies
Are heaved together and
Suddenly
Bleed all over like begonias
The referee is a cabbage white.
Soon one of them drops and
The other is left in solitude,
Shaking in a storm.
Then of a sudden
The world begins to shut like a fan.

MURANO SHIRŌ

Javelin Throw

What is it you are aiming at,
You new primitive man?
Quivering, light took flight —
From the direction it flew in
A sudden horrible scream.
Look, a being
With a javelin stuck in his back, trying
For a moment to escape and tottering —
However, in a short while, everything
Calms down again.

Nobody knows really
Whose face it is.
It is thrust into a world apart, as if,
For example, into the deepest depths of water.

It neither sees
Nor hears anything.
It doesn't speak of the soul's preferences,
Of the name of God or love of mankind.

The day when the blood of dying
Dyes the landscape,
And the cry of the bulbuls meaninglessly
Rends the universe.

It simply stands twined round with ivy and holly
And powerfully scents
An autumn of being.

Over the Wall

Waving his hand and calling goodbye
He turned a corner of the wall beside us
And vanished from my sight.
He will never come back again.

What will there be on the opposite side of the wall?
What sort of world will begin there?
No one, no one can know.
No words, no fortress, no grave —
Or nobody could ever have climbed over
From his shuddering valley in another territory.

Seen from that side, the globe
Is hollow through and through.

Deer

A deer was standing quietly
In the evening sunlight at the edge of a forest.

He knew. Knew his little brow
Was being aimed at.
But what could he do?
He just kept standing there,
A lovely pose, looking towards the village.

The living instant shines like gold
Against the vast forest's night
That was his habitation.

A Bashō[1] *Motif*

His body grew quite cold.
Stumbling among dog's bones and things,
He sensed the evening loneliness
Turn even paler.

At the entrance to a village, he found the way at last.
A scrawny cow was keeping watch.
There was no sign of human habitation in those houses,
But barbed wire strung out everywhere.

The village has already been occupied
By something.

1. Matsuo Bashō (1644–94): the most influential writer of *haiku*,
with whom this seventeen-syllable verse form first achieved maturity.
His most famous work is *Oku no Hosomichi* (The Narrow Road to the
Deep North, 1689) of which there are several English translations
including one by Yuasa Nobuyuki (Harmondsworth, Mddx.: Penguin,
1966).

Little Poem

Something, like a cockscomb,
Started swaying inside me.
A fullness of blood,
A dignity of flesh.

With every one of my frequent
Vomitings and hiccuppings
It is forced upwards, and soon
Becomes this crown on my head.

All its comical
And shivery shape
Is notched with my experience —
Image of an eternal flame.

Mona Lisa

Wipe that wretched smirk off your face.
Such contortions of thought are meaningless.
Please get out of the way.
We can't see the landscape.
You get in our line of vision.
You always prevent us from seeing
Your background and our foreground.

You are really a bandage on our eyes.
Behind it, and you,
Our eyes are bloodshot.
Behind the veiled fertility
Which you vaguely project
There is no eternity or anything.
But what we want to know
Is the reality of painful change,
Desolate precipices and new bones,
All those things you are hiding from us behind your back.

Perhaps behind your broad facial expression
You are not able to see our own face, but we
Cannot see that landscape of yours.

An Ordinary Dog

The face, as I look intently at it,
Gradually appears to be something that is not
What people call a face:
It is a mere shape, managing somehow,
Through a vague response
To the uncertain thing called master,
To preserve itself, but only just, from nonentity.
Then what sort of a family have I got,
Trying to rear it on milk?

When it turns around and walks away
It looks as if it would vanish into eternity,
But when it comes to an abrupt halt
And turns its face towards us
My family's hearts are very blue,
Because it is absolutely
Nothing like a dog any more.

While I was standing under a blue tree
I heard the cries of a swan being strangled.
I sensed that all the swans in the world
Were then being killed.

While I was standing under a blue tree
I saw clearly
That the earth had suddenly started to run
After the planet Venus,
Like a backward child.

While I was standing under a blue tree
I found that, unknown to me,
The whole universe had turned into
A night of earthworms.

Neighbourhood of a Post Office

Living at the back of a main road
My daily routine was
To write poems and stories,
And from time to time
To take them down a slope
To the post office.
A young woman in charge there,
With a sombre look in her large eyes,
Received them always with a friendly smile.

Within that exile of mine
On the fringes of a heaven in a certain shade of grey,
Everything, except that slope with its elder-brushes,
And this third-class post office,
Seemed less than nothing.

What business was being carried out
Next door to the post office —
Even this was something I could not be sure about.
There seemed to exist, on that site,
Some kind of accumulated junk —
But what was it?
Was it really a house?
A family might well live there.
But if they did, they had no faces.

The whole neighbourhood had a forlorn look,
Hopelessly lost, like my own grey matter,
And all the vital juices of real life seemed gone.

Only a solitary telegraph
Kept on calling *click, click, click* . . .
But what for — and to what?

103   MURANO SHIRŌ

In Company

With his entrails removed,
Testicles dismembered,
Glass eyes fixed in their sockets,
He has been there behind my back
Ever since my father's days,
Covered with dust.

His past has been utterly lost to him.
Nothing is more filled with tenderness
Than that look of his, and yet
No one who enters this room
Ever takes notice of the vague benignity
Of this stuffed bird.

Pale Journey

Wandering a weather-beaten
Wilderness I feel my heart
Pierced by a biting wind.

                   — Bashō

To face up to eternity
There was nothing else for me
But to start on a journey with no end,
Leaving my home far behind.

Passing hedges overgrown
With honeysuckle,
And moving through the shade of small trees
In a village where once
The revolutionary troops had been wiped out,
I found my way leading me on
Beyond the ruined terrain
Commonly called a valley.

Was it perhaps the bone of some dead animal,
Or merely the stump of some tree like a deutzia?
Anyway, suddenly I stumbled and, falling on my knees,
Felt myself collapsing
Into the earth itself, where I sprawled out,
Sinking down to some temple underground.

In the night of this village
Where there was no road, no directions,
A moon-pale conglomeration of flesh and blood,
Cold, kept on running.

True, they were human beings,
But they were looking at nothing,
Nor were they being looked upon by anything:
Woods and houses were a clotted gloom,
Standing there stupefied, in solitude.

While I was leaning against
A fence planted in the dust
Of this deserted village,
I heard, coming from beyond the fields,
Sounds as if of an ox being slaughtered —
A strange moan, indescribable.

deutzia: the Japanese *utsugi* is the *Deutzia scabra*, one of the hardiest
species of the genus *Deutzia*; it is a tall deciduous shrub, producing
clusters of white flowers at the tips of the branches in late spring.

Poor-looking Dog

Where a poor-looking dog was standing
Came another poor-looking dog —
From where I do not know —
And, walking up to him,
Smelt all around him —
That was all.
Then, casually, he turned round and
Went trotting away.

Whatever was it trying to do? I wondered.
The incident had something about it
That could not be called a mere coincidence.
— And yet, what an airy, insubstantial encounter!
Nor could the dog ever have been called
A scientific dog, like a space dog.

Soiled and dirty as if
Suffering from abysmal poverty,
Trotting away
He disappeared into the darkness.

When was it? The two of us
Went to some eating-stall
With a view of desolate fields.
We ate small livers broiled on skewers
And then we parted.

That was the last I saw of him:
He is dead now.
A single man, he went to the front
And has been missing ever since.
My memory of him, whenever I come
To this place, as I do now, with its view
Of desolate fields, shrivels smaller every time.

Youth

That voice leaping from afar

Is like the breath of a young mother sleeping,
Smelling of milk —

Like the voices of children at play
On branches wet with sunny rain,

Or like the desolate sound of waves
On some unknown, dreary shore —

That voice from afar so penetrates me,
Transforms me into one of the robed furies —

On the brink of a large, dark pond
Endless flowers are dropping in the water.

The Castle

At times, when I was tired out,
I would have this vision
Of a castle-like object.
Motionless, a figure suggesting conflict,
It would stand in space on the verge of collapse.

On occasion I would imagine
There could be heard coming from it
Sounds like the weeping of women.

Because no one had ever been there
For ages and ages,
The way to the place was concealed and overgrown.
Yet no one forgot the thing was there:
A castle of solitude, leaning
Into distant spaces
Where its tragedy proceeded inexorably
And always defying decay.

Blind Spring

In spring
A lonely journey from the village
Under the smilax bushes.

My dog, of ignoble birth,
Is nameless:

"You, dog, stricken with scabies —
Spectre of a scratchy disease,
You shall drag me on a far journey
Through strange lands."

Through the eyes of countless men,
Through many captive things,
We shall pass through empty hospitals —

And when we reach a hill
We shall have the squirming sea in view.
When you stop
And briskly scratch your back —

That scrubbing sound shall drift on many winds,
The sense of an incurable itch
Shall pass over eternal undulations.

smilax: the Japanese *sarutoriibara* ("monkey-catching briar") is *Smilax china*, a tall climbing thorny shrub.

111   MURANO SHIRŌ

Sewer

Why is it that
Simply by softly whispering this word
My blood is soothed as if
Some poison had met its antidote?

Sewer, hidden exit to hell
Where bits of miscellaneous deaths
Or shrivelled loves or excreta all drop
And start flowing sociably to some place unknown.

It is unnecessary to try to find out
The destination of all those lost futures;
They may perhaps lead to the caves at Cumae
Or go under the earth to the beaches of Malaya —
Anyhow, they will find an exit at some forlorn place
On the other side of the world.

Starting from shit-holes beneath our notices,
Under the daily misery of the streets we tread
This sewer goes on its sodden way, to reach the bowels
Of some strange cities or of cathedrals,
Secret exit of the civilized pariah

And yet, some day when
Our empire crumbles down in flames,
From that irremediable encroachment
Shall suddenly leap out into freedom
A pale king
Crying: "Urania!"

MORI MICHIYO
(b.1901)

Cobra Dancing

An old man sitting on the grass
began to play on a pipe made from a dried gourd.

Out of the flat open basket there came a cobra
lifting a head so flat, it seemed to have been smashed like that,
bringing itself further and further out
as if searching for something.

Sliding out on the grass,
it rocks itself to the old man's music.
Does that melody contain some old song of the marsh
the cobra used to live in?

The sad melody sounds plaintive,
like some sad history told in detail
in a thin, complaining tone.

Once the sadness is established,
the cobra rocks its head from side to side
like an old woman listening at home to an ancient tune, or
like a man in adversity drowning his sorrows in drink.

NAKANO SHIGEHARU
(b.1902)

The Seashore at Kitami

The offshore waters are sunk in a dense fog
The beach is soaking
On this drenched beach a black shadow is moving
The black shadow goes holding a hand-net
The black shadow lifting his net to find only a meagre catch
Who can that black shadow be
Where did that black shadow come from

The catch will always be poor
It must be a cold spot
With little for wives and children to talk about
Will he sell his catch
Will he have any money left over
No
Silently he will move northwards and ever northwards along this
Holding a hand-net
Taking his wife and children
But without domestic animals of any kind

Before long a railway will be running here
Big buildings will go up and
Tall chimneys emit black smoke
Wild greasy shouts of joy will sound
When that day comes
Where will this black shadow be
Where will his sons and daughters be
Will they perhaps have fallen sick
And if so will there be any doctor
Perhaps they will have to die.

Where did this black shadow come from
The black shadow is soaking

Your Song

Don't fetch your song from trembling grasses or wings of
    dragonflies,
or from whispering of winds or scent of a woman's hair.
Put away all that is frail, all that is flickering, all that is sad.
Put all sentimentalism away.
Let your song flow from your honest thoughts, from what makes you
    live, from the turmoil in your heart.
Sing such songs as will retaliate unjust assaults,
Sing such songs as will uplift you out of the abyss of shame.
Sing those songs at the top of your voice,
Sing those songs from the bottom of your heart
      in a pounding rhythm
      beating them home into every heart to come!

The Governor

I got on a train, carrying a small bundle and an umbrella
Then I saw a great crowd such as I'd never before seen on a
 platform
When the train began to move they all bowed together
Public officials businessmen geisha
Directing my gaze towards the focus of their attention
I saw a middle-aged man surrounded by his family
I asked who he was
And learned he was the governor on his way to a new post
I understood then what it was to be a governor

KUSANO SHINPEI
(b.1903)

The Death of Glima, a Male Frog

Glima, fished up and stamped flat by a child, has died.
Widowed Lurida.
Fetched a violet.
Put it in Glima's mouth.

After sitting by his side for all of half a day.
Lurida returned in anguish to the water.
There the others' cries of bliss benumbed her bowels.
Tears gushed in her throat like fountains.

Holding the violet in his mouth.
The violet and Glima.
Withered in the scorching summer sun.

Mount Fuji

Spring light flooding the surface of the river radiant and dazzling.
In a faint breeze lights play blind-man's buff and the leaves of
    reeds talk in whispers.

A reed warbler sings.
On the reed warbler's tongue the light of spring.

In a clover meadow by the riverbank.
I lie resting my chin on my hands.
As the spring light drenches down I feel a growing languor.
Watching.

Small girls plucking the flowers deftly weaving clover-chains.
They twirl the clover-chains like skipping-ropes.
When they whisk the rope high in the sky Mount Fuji fills the
    arch of flower-chains.
With each turn of the rope Mount Fuji takes a step forward.
Then takes a step back and settles down again in the distance.

Songs of the reed warbler in my ears.
Light on my cheeks.

ONO TŌZABURO
(b.1903)

Tomorrow

The old reeds are dead

And the new shoots are few.
Sandpipers are flocking like clouds across the river mouth.
Wild gales are sweeping the sandbanks where
The spring tides churn up dirt.

In this deserted and disordered landscape
I listen to the wind howling over the wastes of heavy industry.
— Surely something must have gone wrong.
Already it is worse than anything I can imagine.
What I see before me is a ghastly landscape of waste lands
      everywhere,
Without sunlight, without sound,
The indelible shadows of an horizon buried
In iron, nickel, rubber, nitrogen, magnesium.

Monstrous Fish

Like a gigantic black marlin
Of stupendous girth
The huge fish monster
Was dragged from the sea.
They abandoned it, and now
There is no sign of human presence on the beach.

From the gashed stomach
The thing is extruding ropes and gutfuls of
All the small fish it swallowed.
It is impossible to describe how gruesome it is,
To discover that all these smaller fishes
Also swallow fishes smaller than themselves.
The sea, a shimmering, dull leaden grey, seems prehistoric.

Now they have caught it,
They don't know what to do with it,
And its only half-dried-out carcase
Left like this on the endless, empty shore
For year after year after year is still
Giving off the putrid odour of a decaying corpse.

TAKAGI KYŌZŌ
(b.1903)

The Winter Moon

I hit my wife and went out and saw
the moon like ten thousand lanterns.

Over the soft snow after a snowstorm
I am walking with no idea where I am going.

— What is it makes me hate so hard?
When we hate, we are more serious than when we love.
Why now am I starting to feel I love her again?

Everything is like that snowstorm.
When it is over, we see
the moon like a thousand lanterns.

Sick Submarine

The view of the International Settlement
seen through a periscope
might be recommended for inclusion in the new design
of banknotes in the Republic of China.
Russian maidens in black swimsuits are
camouflaged Q-ships.
Sailors who declined the Order of the Crimson Starfish
are transformed into white foam and
wash overboard from their ships.
I pick up an opium pipe from under a gyroscope
and recall the phosphorescence
in the wake of a torpedo our ship was tracking.
However, because I forgot the signals
to be used at sea in contacting our mother ship,
this evening too, the Scorpion violates
the sextant's centre, and
the keel of the old ship writhes in agony
in mud and seaweed.
I take off my life-jacket and give the order:
"Verify with depth-gauge angle of descent of rust-red morale!"

How to Cook Women

To cook women,
First of all, put them on the chopping-board
And slice into three parts.
No knife is needed, you may use your bare hands.
Care should be taken to check
Whether those you wish to cook are young or old.
In the case of middle-aged or elderly ones,
The meat can easily be sliced from the bones.
But it is not so easy to cut up the young ones.
They have a lot of small bones.
You have to pick them all out as carefully as possible.
When all the bones are taken out,
Stroke the meat tenderly with your palms
As if making it into rounds.

People say women,
Especially those who are middle-aged or elderly,
Are not edible, even if you boil or bake them.
That, of course, is not true.
The best way to do them is as a *tempura* dish.
So now let me tell you how to fry them.
You should use plenty of oil.
There is a certain knack to frying them on the strong heat of
        passion
So that they turn out crisp, not soggy.
When you serve them on a platter,
Don't forget to sprinkle evenly over them
The leaves of love, chopped small.
Eat before cold.
That's all.

123   TAKAGI KYŌZŌ

A Skyline — New Year's Day

Let us follow the skyline you, an awkward being, present.
There are no sightseeing buses or signposts here.
But you will find swamps in which you once sank up to the
    chest
And jungles where you used to wander lost.
The summit is still far away.

You are now climbing a cliff.
You hammer a spike into the rock
And tie a rope on it.
You hang yourself upon the rope.
O! You are cast away in a sea of clouds!
Are you floating or sinking?
There is no one but yourself to urge you on.
Do take your time, get your breath back.
Wait for the sunrise.

You are not edible in any way.
(Not true?)
You stick out your chest when alone,
But in the presence of others deflate it.
(No?)
You sell kindness cheap.
You are suffocating under your own titles printed on your
    business card.
(No!?)
You've been worrying all your life
That people never seem to recognize you.
(Only thirty minutes left!)
You were born, slept, woke up, ate, excreted and now you're
    dying.
(Now, the gong!)

To the Sea

You bare white fangs,
Roar, twist upon yourself
And punch the shore.
Why are you so angry?
You are raging at the ugliness of our daily needs, aren't you?
We repeat the word *peace*,
And yet engage in wars, even though without arms.
The Japanese, like animals, are struggling just to stay alive.
You cannot stand us any more, can you?

But today you seem to have forgotten completely your usual ange
And are licking the bare feet of women and children
Gathering round you and playing in front of you.
— They really are frightened to death by the anxiety of living.
Won't you comfort them?

Ladies and Gentlemen,
You must be tired
After such a long ride.
Now we are arriving at the river.
On the other bank of this river lies Hell, our destination for
     today.
Look! You can see a mountain in front of us.
Hell occupies the region round the foot of that mountain.
Don't you feel how peaceful this place is, bathed in warm
     sunshine?
Did you expect spring in Hell to be like this?
Well, now, I'll explain why it is so:
The demons have been on a lock-out strike in the mountain
     for about fifty years now,
Demanding a pay-rise.
So now there are no demons here in Hell.
The dead are released from tortures and hard labour
Which otherwise they would have to endure night and day.
Instead, they are enjoying the spring.

Now there we can see a bridge
And a big building next to it.
That is the customs.
In the old days, there used to be old men and women here
Who would strip the dead of their clothes.
But today, Hell is so bureaucratic
You have to pay the entrance tax they have imposed.
The amount of tax varies according to the quantities of floral
     decorations and mourners
And the amount of funeral monetary gifts of respect.
The more you pay, the less hard labour.

O.K. Tom! Drive straight on, please!
Ladies and Gentlemen, this is First Avenue in Hell itself.
You can see the dead sitting around in patches of sunshine by the
    the roadside.
They are looking at us with inquisitive eyes.
You may recognize some of your own relations among them.
Now to your right, in the woods, you see a fine park.
It was built in memory of the Hill of Needles
And of the Blood Bath, both of which used to be situated there.

O.K. Tom! Drive straight on, please!
Oh, stop just a moment, Tom, please.
Here we are now on Third Avenue of Hell proper.
That gorgeous building you see in front of you
Is the Government Centre.
Inside, the Emperor passes judgment on the dead.
But today his status is just symbolic.
Just now, I expect he is weeding his lawn in the back garden.
The next building is the Museum.
Here they preserve and display such things as
The iron batons which demons used to carry
And the tiger-skin breech-clouts they used to wear.

Ladies and Gentlemen.
I wonder if you've noticed that
Despite this busy traffic
Not a sound is to be heard?
That is how this place differs from ours.
But if you listen carefully
You just may hear the dead murmuring.
We are sorry not to be able to show you any demons
After you've come all this way.
No! No! Here they come!
Look over there.
That's a demons' demonstration!
They are coming zigzagging towards us.

It's no good! Demons are demons.
We cannot be too careful when they're about.
Sorry now but we'll have to go home.

O.K. Tom! Turn round and go back, will you?

TAKENAKA IKU
(b.1904)

A Happy Crucifixion

Lying back in bed with one of my children,
I wonder;
> Is he a pigeon?
> Is he an organ?
> Is he a vein of ore?

Fly, my dear, if you are a pigeon!
Sing if you are an organ!
Glitter if you are a vein of ore!

I'll never complain about the narrowness of this bed,
Nor will I mind these difficult hours of night,
As long as I am bound to this throbbing wooden pole,
My limbs numbed with pleasure,
In a happy, happy crucifixion.

IWASA TŌICHIRŌ
(1905–74)

My Mind

Friend,
My mind is well-buckets
Tied to both ends of a rope.
When overflowed
With blissful
Smiles,
My other mind
Sinks deep down to the bottom
Empty.

But
I do not care.
For I know
When delight vanishes
From my present mind
My other mind
Will be hauled up
Drawing fresh smiles
From the deep bottom.

Waking

A milk-tinged
Daybreak dream of mine
Heartlessly you rob me of
With your sudden kiss
So
In my startlement I chase
Sleep flying away like a dove
Longing to crawl once more
Back between my warm quilts
But my efforts were in vain
For with your sharpshooting kisses
Like machine-gun fire
Dream and sleep were accurately shot to death
Reluctantly I open my eyes
One after the other like heavy iron doors

Good morning . . .
Your mischievous black eyes
Are gazing at my wakening
Watching me steadfastly and as if for ever
Then like underwear
Quickly I put my ego on
And firmly
Firmly button my consciousness
. . . Good morning . . .

Gazing at me armoured thus
You begin to laugh again
Like a fresh white rose
Voiceless and windblown

NAGASE KIYOKO
(b.1906)

Mother

My mother haunts me, filling me with a sense of sadness,
something like a strange obsession, and brings me
constant pain in the innermost depths of my being.
She is so frail and fragile as a shell, and yet
I cannot escape from her shadow that I was born with.
Like a dear old nightmare, she plays on my nerves
even when I am awake.
I cannot even go anywhere I may wish to go, for fear,
she might be carelessly broken by my slightest movement,
and sting me sharply, giving me real pain beyond my power to
      stop.

My Harvests

I am a sickle
That reaps this flaming harvest in the fields.
So I cool all my passion and all the fury
I still feel for this world.
After half a year's dumbness and frustration
I lash out with my sickle at
This flaming corona.
No one is watching me —
Only the sky is watching in its empty cavern of brass.
Quickly, breathing hard,
I grasp with my hand and then release —
At this moment, I am a woman from the start of time.
I bring my own solutions.
Within these waves of fire endlessly spreading
I am absolutely on my own,
But one with the millions of this earth.

The barley now is waving its radiant little crests
Of pride, astonishment, rebellion, loneliness —
Swaying, quivering, playing its music
On golden strings — now is the time for me
To play upon them with my sickle,
To be a woman nothing can overcome,
Knowing the pangs of all passion spent
That make us tremble with such strange despair.

But if I do not lash out like this,
My labour cannot sweat my pain away.
This is my act of protest against the smug and prosperous —
Or it could be just an insect habit of mind.
My blazing harvests burn now ever brighter,
And when I shoulder the sheaves in the setting sun
They scorch my back, my fingers, and even singe my hair.

NAKAHARA CHŪYA
(1907–37)

Korean Woman

A Korean woman's flowing ribbons on her national dress
Are not entangled enough to suit the autumn wind.
Whenever you pass along the street
Dragging your small child by the hand,
The parched skin of your sunburnt forehead
Wrinkled in a frown,
I wonder what thoughts lie behind your face.

Yes, indeed, I too have come down in the world.
You give me a suspicious glance — I think
I was watching you in an absent-minded, foolish way —
And move on, dragging your child . . .

A little dust is rising in your wake,
As if trying to tell me something —
A little dust is rising in your wake,
As if trying to tell me something . . .

In the autumn night, somewhere far, far away,
There is a dry river bed of small pebbles only,
And there is sunlight streaming on it —
Sarasarato sarasarato.

As it is sunlight, it glitters like silica or something,
Like the scattered powder of something immensely hard,
And that is why it is making this far off rustling sound of
Sarasarato sarasarato.

Well now, just at this moment a butterfly alights on a pebble
And casts upon it a faint but unmistakable shadow.

And soon, after the butterfly has vanished, unnoticed by us,
Over the dry river bed where nothing was flowing
The water begins to run and ripple —
Sarasarato, sarasarato.

sarasarato: an onomatopoeic expression that suggests the sound of water running.

Frogs Croaking

Heaven envelops the earth
Where there happens to be a pond.
In this pond, frogs are croaking all night long . . . .
— What is the meaning of the sounds they croak?

Will these sounds, that come from heaven,
Return to heaven also?

Heaven envelops the earth
And the croaking of frogs moves upon the waters.

In this country, too, there is too much humidity
For our tired hearts to bear.
We lean against a pillar we think is cool and dry
But our heads become heavy, our shoulders stiff.
And always when night comes the frogs start croaking.
The sounds move upon the waters
And reach the heaven's dark clouds.

TAKAMI JUN
(1907–65)

Old Starfish

You say I'm too grotesque even to be stamped on
and suggest I should be cast back into the sea.
Such pitying contempt is really more than I can stand —
I, a once-admired star of the sea.

I used to be disliked because I ate shellfish.
I used to be rejected because of my inedibility.
But now I am neither hated nor condemned by you.

Now I am plump and shaped like an open flower,
my character harmonious,
all my points broken off
and my star-like arms torn.

Suddenly I found myself in a net,
which made me weep with sorrow for myself.
But soon, thinking it over,
I decided it was all for the best.

For I have been living a disgraceful life all these years,
nibbling oily seaweed, because my loss of teeth
prevented me from eating my favourite dish —
shellfish.

I'd rather lie here on the scorching sand
awaiting the moment of death,
writhing in agony,
recollecting the glories of the past.

That was long ago
when the stars used to shine like so many jewels.
Now they are like white lice
clinging to the dirty sky.

The dignity of Sea Star is already a thing of the past.

Don't cast me back into the sea, but
give Old Starfish a slimy death right here —
please!

The Extra-fine Quality Label

Look, that's where you are going,
that building there furnished with our proud hygienic facilities
like those in a hospital.
So you should enter it in a proper manner.
When you leave it, you will have been changed
into a beautiful commodity decorated with
our extra-fine quality label,
the design of which has strained our ingenuity,
the printing of which has cost us much money.

Naturally you wouldn't want to die a cruel death.
I tell you this is the very place for you,
you, a modern man, with a taste for cruelty,
cruelty to others, but not to yourself.
So you can enter here with your heart at rest.
Or would you prefer to have your skull cracked open with a
        block of wood?
Your body skinned and hung upside-down
to be chopped up and sold at the butcher's?

You don't want to be canned, do you?
We are quite ready to grant whatever you desire.
What method of extermination would you prefer?
We value the liberty of the individual, you know.
You are at liberty to choose whatever method you prefer.
So hurry up and tell me now, you dirty pig
swilling greedily on every thought —
hey, hurry up and tell me!

AOTA MITSUKO
(b.1907)

Under the Tree

Here we have a huge tree hundreds of years old, but
the man who planted this spirit of stillness has
long since passed away.
Time too has passed away,
seasons have rolled away, and
these people I see today
are certainly not
those I saw yesterday.

One day
I saw a young man under the tree, and he, though unable to
talk with men, was talking and talking to the tree.

He was a lunatic, so I was told.

Now, more than ten years later,
I see in the same tree
many insects swarming,
living at leisure
a lifetime's summer.

Where has that young man gone?
Was he really a lunatic?

Only this tree could say.

KINOSHITA YŪJI
(1914–65)

Song of a Winter Night

Quiet night is all around me
as I lean against my loneliness
as if against a scarred desk.
The north wind, which was crying all day long, is now
gone away somewhere; that fierce being of rage and sorrow
also has its own place to go and rest in.
This thought makes me warm wanting to rest too.

A Night's Lodging

I take off my dirty undervest
as if I were shedding my grubby youth.
I put on a fresh one,
sniffing its fragrance of field flowers on a fine day.

Night brings rain, which,
as if it were my mother, waits under my window
till it sees me put my light off and go to sleep.

Voice and Wings

Water said to Clouds: I was once clouds myself,
with huge wings like yours.

Clouds said to Water: I was once water myself,
with a clear singing voice like yours.

I, Like a Tall Tree

I, like a tall tree, have a natural sense of balance, though I
    lean to one side.
I have deep roots on which I take my stand and stay myself
    with.
I grew a tough bark to keep me comfortable — neither too hot
    nor too cold,
I have branches for reaching out to touch my fellow trees,
And green leaves to sway with laughter.

I weave soft shadow-mats for lovers in the afternoons,
And I stow them away at evening in my thick trunk,
From my unchanging height I wave as I see them off —
Lovers leaving me alone in twilight.

I have fragrant airs and flowers and a glittering lake
To tame the young fleet steed of the wind that rushes into
    morning
I have a blue sky for my dreams,
A night sky for starry thoughts,
And an annual ring to encompass my identity.

I have everything yet nothing.
I have everyone yet am entirely alone.

AIDA TSUNAO
(b.1914)

Legend

We catch the crayfish that crawl
out of the lake,
tie them up in straw ropes
and carry them
over the mountain,
to sell them in the stony lane
of the market.

Some people eat such crayfish.

Hanging on the rope,
their ten hairy legs
scrabbling at the air in vain,
the crayfish are sold,
bringing us some money
to buy a handful of rice and salt
when we go back to our home
by the lake.

Here
the grass is dead,
the wind is cold,
our cottage is without light.

In the dark
we tell our children
again and again
the old tales our fathers and mothers told us,
who also, as we do now,
caught crayfish from the lake,
carried them over the mountain
to get a handful of rice and salt
to feed us children
with a bowl of hot gruel.

In time, we also will carry
our own thin little bodies
just as they did, to the lake
lightly,
lightly,
and throw them away in the water,
where the crayfish will devour them,
just as they devoured our parents'
long ago.

That is precisely what we wish.

When the children fall asleep,
we steal out of the cottage
to row out on the lake
which is dimly lit,
to make love
tremblingly,
tenderly,
in agony.

147   AIDA TSUNAO

Wild Duck

Don't be a wild duck
was what the wild duck said
at that moment

No

When we were about to leave the tarn
over which an evening mist had started falling
licking our lips
after devouring the broiled flesh
with its feathers plucked out
with its down singed

"You can still
suck the bones"

We looked back
and saw the laughter
and the shining keel of the wild duck

ZIKKOKU OSAMU
(b.1915)

On the Shore of Night

On the shore of night
a fire burns

beyond the realm of sleep
where the stream of time runs louder

against the darkness
a fire burns alone

devouring one after the other
scraps discarded by the day
soundlessly spreading abroad

shuddering wildly
at its own stupidity

hopping dancing jumping on tip-toe
to reach beyond the darkness

it burns burns burns unquenchable
the flame of my own being!

From time immemorial
everywhere on the shadow-side of earth

has every one of us been burning like this
to burn himself out?

the depth of darkness before day . . . .

In the Sweated Heat of Night

Stomach churned with anger
Inflamed with pain
Bronchi the battered branches
Of dead trees choked by exhaust gas,
Penis standing or falling,
Ejaculates empty pleasure,
Brains burnt to ashes
On strange piles of iron skeletons,
Throat hoarse with streams of lics,
Hand crooked with greed cannot flex,
Legs swollen with flattery,
Torments blasting the whole body —
Yes, this is NIPPON!
Yes, this NIPPON is myself —
Just look at you!

That realization is my only strength,
And I must hold on tightly to it
As I wallow in the sweated heat of night.

NAGASHIMA MIYOSHI
(b.1917)

A Winter Bird

Stepping on the ice
I glided away making no sound
A lone cold needle
On a record
Once having put foot on it
I am a song without end
A lonely winter bird
The white thermometer is frozen like an icicle
In its thin marked tube
My red blood
Goes up and down   today and tomorrow
But then   how far
Shall I have to glide on
Bang   In a fevered world the needle stops
Then God's hand reaches down
To grab me by the scruff of the neck
But since I am a rare bird a protected species
God   pray wait a little while
In the world of ice
Till I close my hot heavy lids.

TŌGE SANKICHI
(1917–53)

At a First Aid Post

You
Who have no channels for tears when you weep
No lips through which words can issue when you howl
No skin for your fingers to grip with when you writhe in torment
You

Your squirming limbs all smeared with blood and slimy sweat
	and lymph
Between your closed lids the glaring eyeballs show only a thread
	of white
On your pale swollen bellies only the perished elastic that held
	up your drawers
You who now can no longer feel shame at exposing your sheltered
	sex
O who could believe that
Only minutes ago
You were all schoolgirls fresh and appealing

In scorched and raw Hiroshima
Out of dark shuddering flames
You no longer the human creatures you had been
Scrambled and crawled one after the other
Dragged yourselves along as far as this open ground
To bury in the dusts of agony
Your frizzled hair on skulls almost bare as heads of Buddhist
	saints

Why should you have to suffer like this
Why suffer like this
What is the reason
What reason
And you
Do not know
How you look nor
What your humanity has been turned into

You are remembering
Simply remembering
Those who until this morning were
Your fathers mothers brothers sisters
(Would any of them recognize you now if they met you)
Remembering your homes where you used to sleep wake eat
(In a single flash all the flowers on their hedges were blasted
And no one knows where their ashes lie)
Remembering remembering
Here with your fellow-creatures who one by one gradually moving
Remembering
Those days when
You were daughters
Daughters of humankind.

To Miss . . .

_____

You live on deep in the ditch of an alley in the slums
At the bomb-blasted site of the Transport Corps
The stony road haunted by a vision of horses
Kicking the air above their torn bellies.

Only a year ago, rainy days would allow you to go out
To the hospital, because you could hide then behind your
    umbrella.
But now you never come out to expose to our view
The memory of that flash the shadow of the B 29
That thundered down upon your face your eyes your nose

One arm ripped away by an avalanching house
The other remaining for you to make your living by . . .
What sad stitches you keep knitting day by day
When bitter blood stains your fingers
In this quiet corner of the town
Humming softly with windmills
The voices of children playing in vegetable plots.

Never have I dared to call on you.
But today I am coming to see you
Along this ruined path.

Welts like serpents
Your skin's sickly lustre baldly naked
Bring back to me my native feelings of compassion for you
As you sit there before me caked with oozing pus
In this hole of constant pain
The heart once of a tender girl now shrivelled to a stone
In the rosy light of the setting sun.

O let me tell you now my dear
Of this burning wish we have that wells up from our souls
Of this passion fierce enough to melt the coldest heart
Of the desperate battle in which thousands of your pictures
Shall overcome the powers of darkness in the world

(Under the droning shadows that even now
Keep looming over us again)

Of that hard-won moment when
Our indignation
And your curse
Shall open into radiance of loveliest flowers!

The Night

Eyes aching
Brimming
In the swarming lights of Hiroshima
Everywhere the swollen scars
On shiny keloid skin
Wet streaks writhing
Muddy mazes stinking of decay
Blasted trunks dotted with flabby buds
And sunk in the drizzling rain
Women's eyes redder than the fires of their cigarettes
Their branded thighs laid open to the view.

O Hiroshima
Sterile erection shattered by an atomic bomb
Women are barren
Men shoot listless sperm
While in that resplendent area of leasehold land
The bowers of Hijiyama Park
The tail-light of a gliding limousine is being born
From the arc lamps of the A-Bomb Casualty Survey Centre
In the air of night
That throbs with New Mexican jazz.

(In window-frames across the river
Feral women are languorously stretching
Removing their petals
Discarding their pistils
As they make ready for nightwork.)

On the roof of the station cradling blinded trains
Mindless characters are spilling from the electric newsflash
Telling of second, third, hundredth A-bomb tests
To the bleeding apparition of a drunkard
Shambling away out of nowhere
The lank shadow of a soldier rising
In a boat scraping the rocks of the black river
When the tide of evening floods the banks
Effacing the footprints left by scrap-metal pickers.

Listen
Dark-blue flutterings disturb the heavens
Across the night towards the dawn
Or from the dawn towards the night
Over Hiroshima's leprous map of lights
Some hanging in the distance
Some suspended suspended half-way
Some trying fearfully to forget
Some desperately seething
Some trembling
Some dying
Crawling on their own blood
Retreading from the doomed memory
The sad nebulae of Hiroshima
Mute and sunken in

The darknesses of history.

Always we have this burning vision:

A city on the delta of some volcanic island, where
The windows of buildings are blazing with colourless flames
    of fire
Traffic signals trapping fire-robed refugees and then
Releasing them again
The big station clock obliterated buried in fires from chimneys
Fire-cargoed ships sailing in and sailing out from the piers
And with sudden soundless hoots of fire
Desperate expresses dragging forth phimoses of fire
Women nestling the fire of pus in their crotches
And when a foreigner walks by striking his lighter
Many beggars in black scuttle after him for alms of fire
Behold that man scavenging a fire-tipped cigarette-end over there

Always we live with this flaring vision of a fire that
Never dies
Never is extinguished.
And is there any one of us who could deny
That all of us are already all on fire?

At night, above the floods of radiant lights
The sheet upon sheet of dazzling neon
I sense a sea of flames heaving up into
The dark tunnels of the midnight skies
Thronged with our disfigured brothers
Feet upon feet hands upon hands
All blood and licked by the cruel tongues of fire
Splintered brains
Galaxies burning at the stake

Collapsing
In roses of fire in blue bowers of sparks
Whirling gales of firestorms
Out of darkness screaming
Indignation regret resentment grief
Curses hatred pleadings wailings
Until all these moaning voices stream from the earth into the sky.
No longer are we what we used to be, ourselves, but other beings
With our own bodies still, but with a burning stink,
With peeled skins bald heads we go
Branded with all the marks of the Atomic Tribe
Humans bereft of the right to live as humans.
Now even a test on some lagoon in the farthest reaches of the
        oceans
Makes us jump
For we know each bomb is hanging on its parachute of
        blackness
Over our melting-pot.

Watch the way the tongueless flames are dancing
The lungless tongues are writhing
Teeth piercing lips
Lips spouting liquid fire
And how these voiceless fires storm through all the earth to
        bring
A blazing Hiroshima to London
A blasting Hiroshima to New York
An incandescent Hiroshima to Moscow

Watch how the voiceless fires go dancing round the world
With gestures of pain and indignation.
Yes, we are all fires blazing with the vision that we fuel
Like forests of furnace fire
Like seas of liquid fire
Lapping the earth in flame and fever.

Yes, we are nothing but a mad mass of fire
Blazing passionately against the next scheme
Of the devils of nuclear holocaust.

MITSUI FUTABAKO
(b.1919)

Looking Back

What are these things left in my hands?
    Birds' bones, old shoes, frayed gloves.
And what's that hanging like a kite
trapped in a corner of that panorama?
    My extinct meditation upon the love I had.
O. how quickly they passed — showers, crowds, youth
and war — making our shocked brains a chaos of snapshots.

Now, look! They have all vanished round the farthest
bend of broad daylight, beyond the back of the universe,
beyond God's bed — like rainbows, jet planes, mirages —
as if compelled by the magnet of infinity.

KURODA SABURŌ
(b. 1919)

I Am Completely Different

I am completely different.
Though I am wearing the same tie as yesterday,
am as poor as yesterday,
as good for nothing as yesterday,
today
I am completely different.
Though I am wearing the same clothes,
am as drunk as yesterday,
living as clumsily as yesterday, nevertheless
today
I am completely different.

Ah —
I patiently close my eyes
on all the grins and smirks
on all the twisted smiles and horse laughs —
and glimpse then, inside me
one beautiful white butterfly
fluttering towards tomorrow.

YOSHIOKA MINORU
(b.1919)

Still Life

Autumn fruits
That grow in brightness
Within the solid frame of the vessel of night
Apples and pears and grapes
Each of them
Posed one upon the other
Sinks into slumber
Into a single melody
Moving along towards great music
When each has attained its utmost depth
The kernel gently settles down
Surrounding them
Is a luxuriant age of decomposition
Now before the teeth of the deceased
They are quiet as stones
These fruits
Gather weight all the more
Within the deep vessel
In this night's semblance
Once in a while
They tilt sharply

First of all the man hangs an apron round his thin neck
The man has no past as he has no will
With a kitchen knife in his hand he starts to walk
Near one corner of his wide-open eyes a line of ants running
Illumined by both edges of his blade the dust on the floor
      begins to stir
If what he has to cook
Is a single stool
The object will undoubtedly scream
Blood will spurt at once from the window towards the sun
Now what awaits the man calmly
To give him
The past he has not had
Is a perfectly still stingray lying on the kitchen bench
Its back is broad spotted and slimy
Its caudal appendage seems to reach deep into the basement
Beyond it is nothing but roofs of winter rain
The man quickly rolls up the sleeves of his work jacket
And plunges the sharp-edged tool into the stomach of the
      living stingray
No resistance
In the slaughter
No defiance
A clean hand is a horrible thing
But the man exerts his strength little by little and rips open
      the filmy space
Obscure depth that has nothing to vomit
Stars that appear sometimes and fade away
When the work is done, the man takes his hat from the wall
And goes out of the door
From the part that had been hidden under his hat
From the nail that is armoured against fear
Trickle drops of blood that have the weight and roundness of the
      whole of time.

164   YOSHIOKA MINORU

NAKAGIRI MASAO
(b.1919)

A Poem for New Year's Eve

It is the last night,
a dark gorge fronting the first day,
and here I am with the softly falling snow
and wild animals far away, while the night
is moulding itself into something indefinable,
and everything around me is cold and miserable.

A little unhappiness taps at the window-pane
and man's eyes gleam in a sadness of ashes
as the last song covers the earth and
the sacred moment is approaching through the dark.
Is there anything left for us to finish
before the moment falls upon us, the tiny point
in the whole span of "Time", the instant when
life and death become one?

O, at that sacred moment,
we are simply aware that
all great sayings have already been said, and that
promise of life is nothing but another form of the promise
        of death.
O, at that sacred moment,
the entire future will flow in
through the door wide open to the tomorrow,
flooding the brilliant room with crystals and beams of darkness.
O, at that sacred moment
I shall forget everything and be forgotten by all, and
just as a corpse falls into a grave
I shall fall into myself,
into the deep and narrow straits of my existence,
into the dark tomorrow of my existence.

ISHIGAKI RIN
(b.1920)

Catching at a Straw

At the end of the morning's work
I go to my firm's gigantic restaurant
and just as I pick up my chopsticks to start my lunch
the background music strikes up right behind my back.

The music has no kind of melody
that would passionately address itself to the human heart
nor any harmonies to grip it with ecstatic sadness,
but only such nondescript veils of tone
carefully chosen, deliberately intended to soothe the workers,
selected scientifically to sugar their fatigue
to stimulate their taste-buds for the tasteless food.

Whenever that insidious music starts
with its lulling melodies like lullabies
washing over the restaurant
I wake up
and get restless –
remembering, as music dandles me,
some scholarly research I read
about how cows when fed to the strains of gentle music
start giving better milk.

In recent years
our industrial giants have evinced
such unfathomably kind consideration for
their workers and for humanity
that I often feel as if
I found myself sinking in bottomless waters –
and suddenly I start fighting free of the tugging depths.

Oh I am drowning   drowning   drowning
in these ever-so-kindly waves of music
drowning
unless I snatch
at the last straw —
my own humanity!

To Live

How could I live without eating?
The only reason I've kept on living is
that I could stomach rice
and vegetables
and meat
and air
and light
and water
and my parents
and my brothers and sisters
and my teachers
and money
and incidentally my heart.

I wipe my mouth
above the discarded bits of carrot
chicken bones
my father's bowels
all cluttering the kitchen sink —

one night — ah, I am forty now,
a beast with her eyes full of tears —
tears that have never been seen before.

Encouragement to Leave Home

Houses are scabs on the earth.
      When our children get boils
      They like picking at the scabs.

Houses are gold brocade and damask.
      Fine feathers make fine birds.
      Evening parties: affectations of the ugly.

Houses are flowerpots
      Providing water, providing fertilizer
      To grow fresh shoots: but roots soon blocked.

Houses are the deadweight of a *tsukemono* stone —
      A little humanity, please!
      Oh my — how sour the taste is!

Houses are pathetic places
      Into which everybody runs
      Carrying their loot.

Houses are cradles of dreams
      But in those cradles
      Praying mantises kill, eat their mates.

Houses are locked combination-safes —
      No unauthorized person
      May force them open.

tsukemono: Japanese pickled vegetables pressurized by a large flat
round stone.

Houses are the graves of everyday
  But people say these places
  Are not what you come to in the end.

And yet people love their houses
  In spite of all this.
  O love . . .

Love is like the scab
  On a child's boil.

So let us all abandon houses —

Let everybody rush outside
And let us play in the wide-open fields
Abandoning our narrow narrow houses
Whose doors it is so important to keep locked.

AYUKAWA NOBUO
(b.1920)

A Story of Heaven

Under the frozen heavens of the November night
He stood with his shoulders bowed
On the deserted platform
A girl with a pale face
Was talking to another girl
      Once there was
      A land called Heaven so I heard
      In it there was a lighted place so I heard

Upon the frozen heavens of the November night
A single star hung glimmering
Just like this girl
He too had to go
Back to a certain place
To a certain place
Dark and cold

      In it
      There was a very beautiful flower garden so I heard
As if wandering through a far-off town
The girl's memory
Seemingly went dark then brightened again

Against the frozen heavens of the November night
Illuminations on neon towers vanished
The invisible thin-bladed knife of the wind
Ripped open the dry skin of the city and was gone
Twelve-ten   the hands of the clock
Look into the heart's darkness
In it there is the expressionless face
Of a woman waiting for his return
With cold soup in front of her
In it
There is an expressionless bed
Crude and wooden

     In it
     There lived a person called God so I hear
Then what had happended
The girl no longer went on talking
Sensing that someone somewhere
Was telling the rest of the tale

Under the frozen heavens of the November night
Two shadows stood close shoulder to shoulder
Frightened of invisible happiness
Reverberations of the last train on the rails
Wheeled round and round in the remote land

MIYOSHI TOYOICHIRŌ

(b.1920)

The Wall

Wall — nightly companion in my solitary abode
To its surface I have entrusted my dreams of the past
On its surface I see strange shadows keep changing their shapes
                       mournfully stretching and contracting.

The wall is sometimes blurred and sometimes clear
On a cloudy day I see a small shadow trudge this way
From a remote corner of the wide field
The shadow becomes larger and larger
(It even appears to have a mouth and eyes too)
Sitting up I clasp his hand that cold palm of his
Tired he says faintly
Changing our places I
Step into the wall.

KIHARA KOICHI
(b.1922)

Revelations

A woman died with thousands of others in the atomic bombing of Hiroshima in 1945 leaving behind her on this earth only a rag of skin but on which the victim's face clearly appeared.

I no longer possess the face of a human being
I am fixed to a fragment of gauze
But that does not stop me from screaming!

Between my teeth uranium lies hidden
In the depths of my nostrils plutonium worms its way
At the back of my sightless eyes helium glares
The world now is no more than a small rock soaked with the
    downpours of raging poisons!

I am a tatter of a burnt human creature
Tranced on this fragment of gauze
From beyond the horizon I hear my lost remains calling to me

Look! Clouds of uranium drive down upon dark seas and shores
Listen! Rains of helium are drumming on dumb windows and
    roofs
But sons of men! Do not let those hands of yours destroy
    mankind
All living creatures are now nothing but plagues of locusts
Moving on unchecked into the waste lands

Beyond

Where do you come from?

From within a blind stone
From within the petals of a rose not yet opened

Where are you now?

Facing a mirror that reflects dying people
Facing a mirror that reflects the newly born

Where will you go?

Somewhere beyond the reach of birds fluttering
Somewhere beyond the reach of fishes diving in the sea

KITAMURA TARŌ
(b.1922)

Dying Light

Bathed
In the slanting rays of the setting winter sun
A dog is sleeping,
His hoary old muzzle lying on
The forelegs stretched on the stone step.

The cruel age dawned brilliantly
On his heavy silver-studded collar
And the heavy chain of all his dark existence:
A sequence of images thrown into confusion, scratched and
        torn
Like everything else in my memory.

February came,
and March is on its way.
(In the stove,
The coals are glowing and quietly rustling.
My master is turning the pages of a history book,
Lifting his rosy face at the withering blasts upon the roof . . .)

April,
Then May.
With my eyes always on the ground
I kept running to every corner of the town
Chasing smells of piss.

June,
And then July.
Yes — I learned many mean tricks
Just to get one scrap of roast beef.

In autumn, the refreshment of water —
The water splashing from the dish
Seemed to cool my fanged animality.

November
and December.

Now in the turnings of endless time,
Bathed
In the slanting rays of the setting winter sun,
With his nose on his paws,
I wonder if it is sniffing the corner of the dream
That is the end of its existence?

Garden

A wintry garden:
Above the quiet dark of cedars and cypresses
There is dark sky.   Various stars
Blaze hard with freezing fires but
       All round me
Everything seems dead.
As I move my foot a little, the brittle grass
Breaks with a snap and
Jars on the bone of deep stillness.

This morning on this garden
A warm sun lavished its radiance,
Condensing a moment in eternity.
The earth's surface hardened by the frost
Bore a dew purer than virgin sweat. And then
I saw
A mantis
Slowly creeping out of the crushed dry grass
And resting on a stone.
There in the wintry light I watched it —
It hardly seemed to know what to do
With its front legs like rusty razors
That had tormented small grubs
In July, with its smell of burning straw.
Its wings seemed to have been torn off
With the rustle of fallen leaves.

The stars burning in the dark sky
Seem closer from any window, or from any bed.
From me, standing in this garden,
They never seemed so far away.
I take shivering steps, slip on an empty
Bottle lying at my feet,
And again gaze at the stars.

Above the cedars and cypresses, the radium of
My heart is slowly impregnated
By the cold of death and silence — where there are
Endless graves of sunset, sunrise.
I reach a certain spot, stop and am silent:
There are countless bodies of mantises run over
By dusty wheels. In that dark sky
Spreads a grove of sighs
And little cries of joy.

At any time, in any place I am all alone,
Unseen by anyone, unseen by the stars
That blaze as they freeze. I am
Simply waiting here, trembling,
Listening to the silence, gazing at the dark sky
In the wintry garden.

TAMURA RYŪICHI
(b.1923)

The Upright Coffin

I

Never touch my dead body with those hands of yours.
Your hands are unable to touch my "death".
Let my dead body be lost in the crowds
In the driving rain.

> We have no hands.
> We have no hands that can touch death.

I know the windows in the cities.
I know the empty windows.
Whatever city I visit,
I have never found you there in your rooms.
Marriage, work,
Passion, sleep and even death
Have all been driven from your rooms
To join, as you have, the unemployed.

> We have no trade.
> We have no trade that can touch death.

I know the rain in the cities.
I know the armies of umbrellas.
Whatever city I visit,
I have never found you were under your own roofs.
Worth, faith,
Revolution, hope, and even life
Have all been driven from under your roofs
To join, as you have, the unemployed.

> We have no trade.
> We have no trade that can touch life.

II

Never lay my dead body on the ground.
Your death can never rest upon the ground.
Let my dead body be placed in an upright coffin
And let it stand upright.

> We have no grave for us on earth.
> We have no grave in which to repose our dead bodies in
>   the earth.

I know death on earth.
I know the meaning of death on earth.
Whatever country I visit
I have never found your deaths in graves.
A young girl's dead body goes floating down the river.
Blood of shot birds, and the many voices of the slaughtered
Are all driven from the earth
To be exiles like yourselves.

> We have no country to live in on the earth.
> We have no country worthy of our death on earth.

I know what worth is on this earth.
I know how worth is lost on this earth.
Whatever country I visit
I've never found your lives filled with anything great.
Barley with its future badly reaped,
Beasts trapped, and your little sisters
Are all driven from your lives
To be exiles like yourselves.

> We have no country to live in on this earth.
> We have no country worthy of our lives on earth.

III

Never burn my dead body in the fire.
Your death cannot be burnt in fire.
Let my dead body be hanged in civilization
Until it rots.

    We have no fire.
    We have no fire in which to burn our dead bodies.

I know your civilization.
I know your civilization devoid of love and death.
Whatever house I visit
I've never found you with your family.
Your father's teardrops
Your mother's painful joy in giving birth, and even the heart
    itself
Are all driven from your house
To be sick like yourselves.

    We have no love.
    We have no love but for the sick.

I know your sickrooms.
I know your dreams festooned from bed to bed.
Whatever sickroom I visit
I've never found you sleeping a real sleep.
Hands trailing from the beds,
Eyes open to something great, and thirsty hearts
Are all driven from your sickrooms
To be sick like yourselves.

    We have no poison.
    We have no poison that could make us cured.

SAGA NOBUYUKI
(b.1902)

Bone

As I had nothing better to do,
I tried removing my skull,
but only succeeded in making myself completely miserable.
What I saw was a white bone six inches long sticking out
from between my shoulders, giving a jerk from time to time.
There was not a trace of the painful passion I once felt for
    someone,
no bird flew down to alight upon it,
nor could I tie to it a tired horse from a distant village.
So I hastily took up the skull and put it back in the old
position, where it set once more on its bone, giving a dull click.
But that extraordinary sound is stuck with me for ever now.

SHIBUYA HARUO
(b.1924)

A Girl in the Street-car

From a black overcoat lightly filled
Her pale neck lines are flowing.
Down the egg-shaped symmetry rising above them,
Rich tangent lines of her long hair hang freshly.

Her body, the head drooping a little,
Is being pressed tenderly by certain unknown forces,
While her hard shoulders are still sheltered by childhood.

Her life, which has already opened in anxiety,
Calls to her, with all her expectations.
Her eyes are so bright
Between what has been done already and
What has not yet started.

Snow

When one more light is piled upon an old mind, the quiet weight is likely to make sounds. I hold up my hand and pursue shadows on the snow. The bird dwells in the sky, drawing huge rings more quickly than the wind. I pick up a stone suddenly and throw it up as far as possible. I throw up my one will to the very end of this white extension.

The sky is hard as rock-crystal. But I hear something like an answering voice from a distance.

Pure bitterness, I hope, will shine in my future smile.

A Stone Pile

This hard, dry mass,
Sticking up in surrounding vacancy,
Disappears completely at times,
Leaving a hole scooped
In this transparent space.

Lemon-coloured coldness
Is intensified and subdued
By its rusty will, leaning a little.

Laughter of old age, strangely
Hardened and plastered,
Is kept silent
In front of me:
A severe fruitlessness.

A Coliseum in the Desert

In the heavy rain
He thinks it a time of music.
Night ascends from the ear like a butterfly.
He drips lonely green ashes
On the plastic spiral stairs,
Then stops outside the door.

She puts a pistol on a flower table on a dark Sunday.
She stands up violently and beautifully from a chair.
Her coral-coloured wet lips,
Her breast engraved with light,
Her swift and skilful smile.

With her charming monkey eyes,
Exposing unlucky loveliness in the rain,
She disappears from a glass door.
He alone hearkens to a useless choir.

Using an axis of his heavy hand
He at a certain moment shines in his frozen jades
A hemisphere of desert, reflecting a bubbling purple glass,
And lets the charming devil in his bosom sleep.

How can we learn the significance of experience?
Planting a flower of complete falsehood,
He strikes, with his incurable yellow nail,
Black keys of funeral out of his double-imaged memory.

A frozen hour clears above gunsmoke.
One tooth projects for ever
From a window where French chrysanthemums are sweet
     smelling

187   SHIBUYA HARUO

With the brilliant shadow of death-premonition,
With the pain of a finely opened fan,
With an exact smile like a weapon.

Chains, more blue than night,
Are dripping from the neck of a violin.
Her delicate animosity counts
The exposure-time of a bleeding rainbow.

His memory treads with vortex shape
sticking to nightmares of light
In a movie ended without any beginning.

"Then who were you?"
"It was your own trap that you called out
And your murmurs are a blue bone stuck to a music."
He is going down first of all with his head bent,
Tying the bellows of pitiful victory round his abdomen.

A woman, a leech.
Behind him, base metal footprints stretch away
And suddenly a cell creaks.
Bass notes like rain
Retreating toward a wharf.

Over him, a damaged ship is bending down like a nail.
They parted at the same angle as a pair of scissors.
A man of death in him
Is still drinking a cup of wine, little by little.
Another man in him
Has gone to the white spinal cord of the city.
Another to a fog-bound dark sea.
Another enters into the feeling of a crow.
A shadow runs through her enchanting cheek
Like a hidden plot, shaded
By the cruel beret of night.

At the end of his vain last movement
His night is opening again like a black fountain.
First bending his fingers,
Then breaking his despair like a piano-string
He stops outside the door.

"How can we learn the significance of our experience?"
Another man in him, his breast all leaden,
Shoots down a grape-coloured portrait of a girl
Without any reason, on the street,
The time, eleven at night.

A Sign

The sky is veiled.
A window is veiled.
A picture-frame, a flower-vase
And all things in the room are veiled.

Things that are always there:
The smooth variety of what is being seen —
A cup of coffee, an opened book
An obsidian ring shining on her finger.
These are all veiled.

Eyes suffused with tears,
Delicately speaking, sliding with a smile,
Flower-buds of light begin to peep out from
The flow of her long hair framing her youthfulness.
These are all veiled.

There comes, however, a certain sign.
The buzz of a horse-fly pierces
Through me in an instant.

It aims at me.
It arrives just a little sooner than I realize
And enters into the world of words.

An old man's wry neck,
And as he walks past the window
His strange, jerking step,
The shadow of his overcoat
Whose wretchedness becomes rather comical
Pierces me through all of a sudden.
Under a little disguise
It maintains its identity obstinately,

190   SHIBUYA HARUO

And on one occasion
Emerges only to disappear.

Something narrower than meaning.
At times it is a grey shadow.
A slight golden glimmer whirling in flower-petals.
It is a beam of light penetrating darkness,
Or like what will produce light.
It draws attention to itself
With its metallic hardness
Amid the easy familiarity of human talk.

At the same time
I have reached already
What was to be signed like the point of a gimlet.

191   SHIBUYA HARUO

Today, spring comes to the city.

Lights are talking
To girls' long eyelashes and curving mouths
And to cherry-petal-coloured ears.

When orange juices are over
Overflowing time makes advances to me.

Light of an agave.
Light of Chopin
Pigeon-clock of one o'clock in the afternoon
Light of the white apron of a waitress.

I make up my mind to write a long letter.

Sensitive trees
Crimson their cheeks.
Something like sweet tides
Pressing up from within them.
Opening their palms
Then, light there also
Has a laughing voice.

Kite-bird
Draws a circle.
Whistle of spring.

Boys cycling
Treading silver pedals
Go dashing into clouds.

Spring has come
Today,
Even to the sweet smell of my pomade.

193   SHIBUYA HARUO

Fragment

In a hospital

When I close my eyes
Huge crosses are blooming
In the counterlight of an evening.

An old mourning-band.
Many blood-coloured flowers open.
I strip off their petals.

An evening.
I wake up casually.
In the window,
Pretty, rotten eggs of clouds
Are sailing past, one after the other.

I want to cut my nails.
Beside my bed
A Russian dancer is smiling
Leaning against a brick wall
In a snowfall in December.

She lowers her head.
I drew her black shoulder again
With my big pencil.

Call to You

My call to you
Rebounds as if in front of a mirror.
We walked together to a certain place.
Then all at once you moved to the other side.
A window confined by an iron bar
Separates us completely.
The dark part of your mind which is called sick
Laughed at me, metallic.
From the afternoon
When a red cockscomb inclines, lonely,
And autumn describes a beautiful blue sphere,
You wandered away somewhere.
You left a white shirt on your table.

From tilting, bad dreams of earth
You departed in a hurry
With the steps of a drunk man.

Then started our rainy seasons.
Blue leaves which will never be sick
Got wet. I think, simply,
This dazzlement is slightly painful.
My hands, having nothing to do, reach out
And shake small flowers
In front of a monotonous grey.

My hands at last find a memory of lilac clouds
And search the faces of our youth
When we were completely cruel,
Cruel in clouds.

195   SHIBUYA HARUO

I call to you.
Am I an actor who cannot exit after the play is over?
No, I want to begin our play again.
Listening to your high-pitched voice
I stand boldly in the heavy rain
That is raining today, not tomorrow.
It casts a cloud against my head.

Now I can say,
Using a small voice,
Looking into the distance,
That I have a healthfulness in my smile
Which you
Never had.

YAMAMOTO TARŌ
(b.1925)

The Missing Word

Our words
Are not within shooting range
Do you realize
Aimed at our hearts they never strike
Soul has been smashed to bits
Retaining none of its original shape
This morning too a word
God
Descended my throat
Like an ice-cold drink
Don't steal glances at my face
It is not my mouth
That opens towards you
It is the remains of caved-in words
Fragments of tusks
Keep on roaring like drifting ice-floes
We utter
Many words
But we cannot recall
The one word alone
Thoughts have many layers
Streams of lava thrust away petrified words
And try to lick truth with the red tip of their tongues
But we mistake it all
For an underground rumbling of fear

What are you afraid of
Do you truly believe
That from the very start we lack
The gift of making one another happy
Don't look back

Even if you do there's no one there
Only a vista of dark holes in a line
Brought to a standstill
Men who talk with their backs
Are very poor
Have you heard
The comical report
From the dead
They cry "Salvation!" "Salvation!"
In our age
The dead are all wrecked ships
They founder in bubbling foam
Words that were shot without a target
Words that are crippled in flight
We may say they are poems
The dead are all poets and poets are all deathbound divers
They are not satisfied even when they reach the bottom
Bubbling foam
They continue to slander
Life that in the final analysis is endless

Prayers and love
Pooh! speak not of "salvation"
Will you let yourself be caged
In such a private system
Wagging a worn-out tongue
Are you going to bury yourself in the tomb of words
Hah! "salvation"
Can you understand the meaning of the word
The meaning of a poem to them
And to us
The meaning of only fragments of words
Recall the one word alone
The word that is stronger more compelling than love
Don't turn away your face

My eyes are perhaps
Gloomier and grimmer than yours
But only face to face
Can we ask each other the forgotten word
Look the landscape is really empty
And the dusk well matches
Our hollowness
When I arise my shadow arises too
When we are conjoined the air is simmering
We are the focal point of sunbursts
Around the flame
Light and darkness overlap each other and quiver
The sharp point of the force that bundles us together
Was invisible round a corner of the block of time
But if anything drags us along we will go forward
The world to us who are under surveillance
Is a far-away concept
And remains there for prayers are non-existent from the very
      start

Recollect that one word
The one word that will reach you
We are not far away

YOSHINO HIROSHI
(b.1926)

To My First Born

One day soon after your birth.

Like vultures
They came
And opened and closed
Their black briefcases.

They were life insurance salesmen.

(What quick ears you have)
To my obvious astonishment
They replied, laughing,
"We got wind of it"

When even your features are not yet formed
Where
Upon your soft body
Have I distributed your little share
Of death?

Already
Its fragrant scent is floating
On the wind   they said.

*Burst**

The business proceeded calmly and smoothly
    infallibly immaculately

    for thirty years

    until there came the day of the ceremony
    honouring those who had served for many years.

Amid the long flowery speeches by the employers
    one of the workers began to cry, his face all white:

—   My friends!
    Let us talk about our souls,
        about our very own souls!
    All this time we have never talked
        about our very own souls!

At the embarassed feet of his fellow workers
    he fell down, wet with a cold sweat.

A flower of madness
bursts open.

—   The same dream again.

*Title in English

KURODA KIO
(b.1926)

Grass Doll

I make a doll
Whose coarse hair whirls
Right down to
His deep dirty mouth
Crammed with teeth like trees.
For his members
I slash off the limbs of a toad.
His palms larger than his body.
His eyes
Mirrors of terror
Pouring doubts like so much mud,
Unconsciously shooting arrows
Always wide of the mark.
I make such a doll.
He has nothing — not even a strip of land.

Burning Giraffe

I heard about this burning giraffe.
I wanted to have the burning giraffe.
I wanted to have the colour of the flame entwining with the
   long neck.
I wanted to have the colour of the fire originally given it by
   some foreign painter.
I myself set a straw horse on fire, which gave only dull smoke,
   leaving an acrid smell of straw ash.
I ran out of doors.
The reason I am crying is not that I am sad but that I am
   worried about that burning giraffe.
But all I can see is the mulberry leaves whose astringency gives
   them a burning colour, and a cat running away from the
   mulberry orchard with a dead silkworm in his mouth.
I can no longer restrain myself, now that I know there is a
   giraffe burning in the world somewhere. I start crying
   for that burning giraffe.
Beyond the mulberry orchard there is a village, where you're
   bound to meet an idiot, sure to walk down the road at a
   fixed hour every day.
But this is the silent hour of summer afternoon before he
   presents himself in the road.
I started to release a desperate shout of defiance to this strange
   silence, rushing to the lookout post hidden at the cross-
   roads, to the bell hanging from the eaves, to the old pump
   behind the door; when I came to the door of my old dark
   prison, I suddenly found myself — the bell madly ringing —
   surrounded by rushing shadows in black who, pointing
   the muzzles of their hoses at me, cried:
Where is the fire?
Here is the fire, sir. I have the fire right here, sir.
You know you are violating the law.

I don't care about the law, sir. All I want is a burning
giraffe.
No sooner had I said this than I was struck by a sharp spear of water
that went right through my chest.

IBARAGI NORIKO
(b.1926)

The Living, the Dead

Living apples, dead apples —
How can we tell them apart
When we stand in the bright shop with a basket on our arm?

Living food, dead food -
How can we tell their tastes apart
As they cook in the hearth, in the mountains, at a restaurant?

Living heart, dead heart —
How can we tell them apart, listening
To fluttering signals, deep silences, echoless dark?

Living heart, dead heart —
How can we tell their truths apart
When the two go staggering along together in drunken peace?

Living land, dead land —
How can we tell them apart
In the slaughters of today just like the murders of the past?

The living, the dead —
Those close companions, always hand in hand,
At all times and everywhere they go, covering their traces —

Covering their traces.

When My Beauty Was at Its Best

When my beauty was at its best
town after town came tumbling down, giving us
glimpses of blue sky stuck up in
the least expected places.

When my beauty was at its best
many people around me died
in factories, at sea, on unknown islands, and
I had no chance to make the best of myself.

When my beauty was at its best
I had no young man bringing me lovely presents.
All they did was raise their hands in salute, and soon
left for the front, leaving me with nothing more than pure looks.

When my beauty was at its best
I was empty-headed,
I was stubborn-hearted,
my limbs were a glossy brown.

When my beauty was at its best
my country was defeated.
"How can that be?"
I strode around the humbled town, my sleeves rolled up.

When my beauty was at its best
I heard jazz streaming from the radio,
and I plunged myself as rapturously into its sweet melodies
as when I first knew the forbidden pleasure of smoking.

When my beauty was at its best
I was very unhappy,
I was very awkward,
I was very, very lonely.

That's why I've decided to live a long time if I can,
like Monsieur Rouault, the dear old man who
painted those marvellously beautiful pictures in his old age.
— Yes, in his old age!

Swimming swimming
Bravely with overarm strokes
With inexhaustible vigour
Swimming everlastingly
Dense layers of water
And the water's resistance to my body
Carve me vividly   So I was able to swim after all
                          yes I am swimming
                          and why shouldn't I be able to swim
Rippled lake in Shiga   no no
Seems bottomless the deep green of the water is ghastly

Oh, that's Kaneko-san! Ka-ne-ko-sa-a-an!
I am kissing the poet Kaneko Mitsuharu
My kiss must have been a terribly fierce one
Kaneko-san yelled Ow!
And turned his face away coldly
Suddenly I seized his legs hung him upside down
And tenderly I kissed his shins
The hairs of his shins were deliciously downy
Kaneko-san laughed loud and happily

My favourite corner of the street
Here it comes here it is
Why was it so difficult to get here
Though I yearned to reach
This acute-angled corner lined with stylish shops
Is this Switzerland
Rugged snow-covered mountains lie in the distance, poignant
The familiar street where I often shopped
Light-heartedly I am selecting pretty papers and small articles
I have no children and

I don't care about the future of humanity
Even if we run around in jungles and escape death
Our remaining life is short
Even if we live to a hundred there is no difference between us
      and nameless birds
That peck seeds from wild thorns and vanish without leaving even
      a trace
Fujiwara Michinaga
In chronological tables your days are compressed into only five
      centimetres
How short is life
Hey, *garçon*, bring me a bottle of *sake*!

Waking I find myself sinking like a hammer in the water
            Kaneko-sama   even though it was in a dream
Please forgive my rudeness
            Where is that corner
Someone else's memory seems to have wandered into mine
            I am bleeding I don't know why
With a glum face
I proceed to the town hall to pay my accumulated overdue taxes
If you fail to pay by tomorrow your telephone and everything
      will be confiscated
That's what they informed me
A bad road a muddy road one has to be prepared for accidents when
      riding on a bus along this road
This is daylight robbery nothing to be gained from it for me

Why are we all so submissive
Being without children
Affects the yesterdays todays and tomorrows of humanity
Persistently
O hydrangeas! they are pathetic flowers
But I like the way they bloom in clumps
We take for granted that
Our heads and bodies during the day are sane but
But

NAKAMURA MINORU
(b.1927)

Winter

The heavens glancing between buildings
Are narrower narrower than the street
ın the depths of those dense clouds
The yellow sun certainly moves

Behind the crowds of overcoats
Always someone is watching me
Every morning in the jostling crowd at the station stands always
        beside me
A man with a different face each day

Closing my eyes I see behind the lids
Storms of snowflakes whirling down
In the last fields where muddy boots have been kicking
Boughs are crucified against the sky

Such moments come on me without warning
Alone, I am cast away upon a street
Abandoned under heavy clouds

— How can I escape at this late hour

TAKANO KIKUO
(b.1927)

Top

Whatever love
Whatever aloneness
You cannot keep going
You keep going
When you are spinning
Upon yourself upon yourself
Yet how have you overcome
Spinning upon
Yourself upon yourself
Whatever dizzy spells
Whatever *la vie*
But
Still even now
Which of us does not
Through such activity
Go on living through unbearable tedium

Hands, You

Hands, you follow
A reverse course
In which all you won
Is let drop
One by one
Until you have
Nothing left.

Hands, you follow
A reverse course
In which you keep losing
Until you have nothing left to lose
But nothingness, and just
Have to fold your empty palms
Intently!

HASEGAWA RYŪSEI
(b.1928)

The Cranes of Paolo

Winnowing strong winds
Urged by a soaring force
Both cutting and thrusting aside
The fogs of space
Thousands of birds migrating
With one and the same oaring of pinions
Vibrations resounding
Deep in the channels of my ears
Are they cranes or storks
It is hard to say
The strange pinion pulsations of Paolo
Vibrantly winnowing and beating
Endlessly down from over the drumskin
On the hushed heavens of the cerebrum of night
Like the thrumming pectoral fins
Of flashing flying-fish.

From a swamp of despair
The strange cranes of Paolo
Have soared out of sight
Whether venturing upon darkness
Or heading for the dawn
They are beginning to wing with vigorous fans
In flocks a hundred strong
With their green beaks uplifted
Each treading on the tail
Of the crane in front
Balancing stresses
Gliding on air currents
Strung out in the long line
Of their flightpath.

The one at the end of the line
Is a deadweight of resistance and fatigue.
But one after the other
The leader is changed
One after the other
The leader flies to the back of the line
Well-balanced
And describing a slight arc
They soar exquisitely
In line through space.

Have you never seen it
Constantly smoothed and shaped
By the surface of the reflecting arch,
The cerebrum of night. Overhanging
The ocean of the occipital cerebral lobe.
Whether bent on nothingness
Or heading for the dawn
The thousands of cranes of Paolo
In flocks a hundred strong
In challenges of migration.
All those hundreds of cranes uplifting their beaks
Each treading upon the tail of the crane in front
Strung out in a long and soundless line
Everlastingly.

SHINKAWA KAZUE
(b.1929)

Never Bind Me

Never bind me
like a bundle of stocks,
like a bundle of leeks.
Never bind me, please; for I am ears of rice,
those acres of golden ears of rice that in autumn
tan the breast of the good earth.

Never pin me up
like some insect in a specimen case,
like a picture postcard from the highlands.
Never pin me up, please; for I am winnowing of wings,
the throbbing of unseen wings that since time began
have always been fanning the reaches of the skies.

Never pour me out
like milk watery with the tedium of everyday,
like lukewarm *sake*.
Never pour me out, please; for I am ocean,
that bitter ebb and flow of boundless water
fabulously overflowing every night.

Never label me
daughter or wife.
Never keep me always planted in that solemn chair
called mother's, please; for I am the wind
that only knows where I must go to find
an apple tree blossoming, a spring.

Never divide me
like a letter laden with commas and full stops and
numerous paragraphs each ending in goodbye.
Never be so pedantic with me, please; for I

am an endless sentence, a one-line poem that
like a river flows and
keeps on flowing and endlessly spreading, spreading.

An Event That Doesn't Make News

Did you see that? In a certain spot in a shady wood
a girl from whose supple arm outstretched there flowed
branches and leaves suddenly changing her into a tree?
Did you see that? A youth who happened to be passing by the
     tree
cast off his dark blue coat to turn himself there and then into
     a dove?

  (Telephone bells are ringing and ringing but
    nobody answers; there is nobody there; this is Sunday.)

When suburban trams light up,
people hurriedly scramble themselves back into
human form and return to the busyness of towns. But
haven't you heard? These days in the outlying pastures
they are always sure of finding a strange horse or two
has been added to their stock following a public holiday.

  (Telephone bells are ringing and ringing but
    nobody answers; there is nobody there; though this is Monday.)

TADA CHIMAKO
(b.1930)

Fireworks

Taunting eternity
loud arpeggio vermilion gold
fern fronds perishing in dissipated shreds
night's flashpoint hysteria.

Song of Kairos

Eyes fixed stare, lips shut tight
I streak through
stockstill phenomena.

No one realizes my approach
of sheer speed
with long hair waving in the wind

or rather my never-ending reachlessness —
Man only recognizes me when I have passed beyond
his calling after me

but I never turn to look behind
nor falter in my stride
for any plaintive cry pursuing me.

Man believes this swift step
never stumbles or fails although
I stand aghast at my own loving compassion.

Quickening my pace I speed past
evoking in these phenomena
nothing but remorse

yet Man can never realize
that I, good fortune personified,
am that flash of remorse

I

I am planted on the ground
As happy as a cabbage.
These verbal weeds I wear systematically stripped away,
My absence will be proved, but also
The presence of the root I am sitting on . . . .

A Dirge

I

Soul, you have only
two colours in your world:
the blue of bottomless skies,
the whiteness of fresh graves on smothered desires.

II

Your silence was already beginning to
stink like Lazarus.
It might otherwise have been a voice that
makes air tremble, luxuriates in
florid language, gradually bears seeds to
drop secretly into the soil of human minds.

III

In the vast reaches of emptiness
shall you still be that individual who
refuses all others and is refused by all others,
a star independent of any constellation?
Even when your flash is agonizingly tugged by
the inescapable might of universal gravity?

221   TADA CHIMAKO

Dead Sun

A child comes crawling into
a world not yet wrinkled, dripping
glistening drops all over.

The child turns a somersault;
an hourglass too is turned, to
mark the start of new times.

The child picks up stars to skim across the waters,
while fish from prehistoric times laugh, waving their fins,
drenching the feet of the gods with their splashings.

. . . .
The child gradually grows up; now
his world full of footprints is
heavy with memories. Then
he gives a long yawn, and
is off somewhere never to return,
with a dead sun stuffed in his pocket.

Morning or Sea
_____

The sea resembles morning
a morning spread out bent like a bow as far as the eye can see
and warblers are dotted about like small islands
sending up spurts of staccato spray.

O breathings that ruffle the surface of the earth
O tidings of an expedition all tails and fins
and of a spindle-shaped dream gliding on the tide!

Winged seeds of grass
impatiently yearning for their white voyages
O how easily
they melt into light.

Everything is overturned and torn away
memory is naked and blind
and then   later on   a fabulous footprint.

Today with its irresistible overflowings
has no seam in it anywhere —
morning resembles the sea.

IRIZAWA YASUO
(b.1931)

Newlyweds

With all the stars turning into grey dogs retreating
I am sitting and you are sitting
Distant cries crumbling temples a gigantic iron rake
At the heart of every tired home the night phantoms are stirring
And within you hundreds of suspension bridges are trembling
     perilously
And you sit with your drowned sisters at your side

With all the stars turning into grey dogs retreating
A white maiden fled with a sailor over the horseshoe-scattered
     sea
I am sitting and you are sitting

At the heart of every crumbling temple old dreams are stirring
And deep within you your drowned sisters call to one another
While you sit laughing at the retreating stars

(Nine spindles are being shuttled from east to west
I am sitting and you are sitting
The spinning-wheel is being spun so fiercely it gives off sparks)

When you turn into my sea-wet wife and all the stars retreat
When grey dogs go running across the fields
One dream ripens into the shape of a full-grown head of wheat.

ŌOKA MAKOTO
(b.1931)

Lacking Even the Merest Shred of Feeling

A poor fellow, whose heart is lacking even the merest shred
   of feeling, is making his way across the wintry Sumida
      towards a universe devoid of birds
         as well as of love.

A poor fellow, whose heart is lacking even the merest shred
   of courage, whose lungs are black with tar, is washing
      his little one's neck in the waters of the Sumida
         aflame in the desperate glow of the setting sun.

I have been travelling on a long journey, whose distance
   I've been counting those thirty years, still not finished,
      always alone
         except for the women offering themselves.

The place I've been trying to get to is perhaps
   a city built of wind,
      an invisible city ever-changing like a kaleidoscope,
         a city of pain where it is men who begin to bear children.

As I can't believe in the good faith of conquerors,
   so I can't believe in the ill will of the people
      who have always been deceived.

      O, for mercy's sake, every one of you,

at least keep yourself away from
the innocent just about to be born!

HORIKAWA MASAMI
(b.1931)

The Voice

The hem of the suspended sky flutters and leaps
And the sky sometimes
Raises its hem
To make quite sure of its being the sky
Then drops it again
To rise even higher

Something born of the heat
And hotter than the heat
Ascends and
Constantly accompanies the widening gap
Between heaven and earth
And birds that never die in any heat
Flutter and fly
Round and about it

He who tanned animal hides with his tongue
Is not necessarily our
Father or Mother

When street walls
Bulge outwards
And fall to pieces
The voice
Extends peacefully
From you
Towards me

The Edge of Night

My place does not lie in the direction towards which the
    tolling of bells fades away.
This involuted world will be unfurled before long.
Somewhere a man like an hour-hand vomits bending forwards.

Well, everybody has fallen asleep. Under the window waves are
    surging,
The languid city is dissolving round the edges
Is being licked and lapped by great tongues.

Climbing to the top of words, beyond the slope
The end of night was seen glittering like a crystal door.
I made my way towards it, crawling slowly.

SHIRAISHI KAZUKO
(b.1931)

Town under a Rainfall of Eggs

While taking a rest in a pool of green lettuces,
we are showered with a rain of eggs —
cheap eggs, dear eggs, hard eggs, soft eggs.
We are showered with babies, boys,
rats, heroes, monkeys, grasshoppers too, falling
on church roofs, on playgrounds.
We hold out our hands in longing, but
they all, like sorrow, trickle away through our fingers,
with a funny top hat
dramatizing the height of a tall building.
The eggs fall through the chill veins of vegetables too.
What for?
(I don't know, don't know, don't know.)

This is the editorial in our town's local newspaper.

*Bird**

BYE BYE BLACKBIRD
It is not hundreds of birds nor thousands of birds
But always one bird only that takes wing from within me
Bearing my ugly guts.
Bird,
Every time I conceive you within me
I am made blind, and live a blind existence
Sniffing my way around the world.
I see you only when I have lost you.
But then I see my old self die and
A new blind self begin to bud.
On stage, He, changing himself into quite a bird, sings:
BYE BYE BLACKBIRD
Attended by the tens of thousands of ears in his audience.
Then the audience becomes millions of blind wings.
The blind audience has turned into so many ghosts of
Fluttering birds, dancing among the dark seats,
Following the crying of the one bird on stage.
So can anyone tell which is the real bird among
All those ghost birds?   And
BYE BYE BLACKBIRD
What can it be, really, taking wing from here?
The singer himself cannot tell, who is just singing
In ecstasy, feeling, now that something is flying away,
That the real entity may be his smooth rhythm, or may be
The softest loin of his soul, or may be the memory of the
Star of guilty conscience, or may be the warm splash of
Blood out of the tulip-shaped brain of the child seated
Right in the front row.

*Title in English

BYE BYE BLACKBIRD
I am a bird,
Whether I refuse to be myself
Or accept,
Just as long as I am not yet deprived of this
Ever-pecking pointed beak and
A pair of naturally fluttering wings,
I am a bird today,
Making myself into a prayer, piercing the sky
Several times a day, only to be thrust down upon the ground,
Or I am the guts the falling bird is bearing.
Here within myself I have gathered all these fallen birds — huge,
Small, thin and dwarfish, arrogant, gentle: some are still half
    alive, moaning.
Every day I perform the bird funeral for them, in which other bird
Strip their flesh to the bones,
While
Every day I warm their eggs so as to hatch out the little ones.
Such eggs I warm all the more lovingly and desperately when I
    know
They will grow into grotesque birds that one day will destory
    our future.
BYE BYE BLACKBIRD
I am planning to make that fellow fly away some day, the one
I know will come back and destroy me; yes,
I must expel him so violently that he is bleeding all over,
And then I can really sing for him with all my heart:
BYE BYE BLACKBIRD

230   SHIRAISHI KAZUKO

YASUMIZU TOSHIKAZU
(b.1931)

I Don't Like It

Oh, please darling stop it for heaven's sake!
Please stop exhibiting yourself bit by bit.
This stawberry-like-wantonness
this fish-like shyness —
stop it for heaven's sake.
The shoulder like a Bible,
the forehead like a mother —
all well and good, certainly.
But why do you refuse to show your all?
Oh, just imagine how beautiful it is,
this vexing murder scene,
this room scattered with all these little bits of you?
True, I enjoy reading detective stories, but
how can I possibly accept
the idea that you have taken part in this, and
are none other than the victim herself?

TANIKAWA SHUNTARŌ
(b.1931)

When I Gaze at the Blue Sky

When I gaze at the blue sky
I feel I have somewhere to go home to.
But the radiance that breaks through the clouds
Can never return to its home again.

The sun is eternally, lavishly spending its light —
Even at night we are greedily collecting it:
Human beings, we all are meanly born,
And can never repose in natural luxury, like trees.

A window frame cuts off all superabundance.
I want to have no room but the universe.
That is why I have become estranged from other men.

To exist means to give hurt to space and time,
And the hurt I give them reflects upon myself.
But if I leave this place, my health will soon return.

Billy the Kid

First fine clay upon my lips then bigger and bigger clods of
earth between   my legs and on my guts   an ant whose
home had been destroyed crawled for an instant over my
shut lid   people have stopped weeping and appear to be
shovelling bathed in healthy sweat   in my chest two bullet-
holes blazed by that sheriff with the doe-like eyes   promptly
my blood pumped from the two mouths   it was then for the
first time I realized that blood was none of mine I knew that
my blood and me hot on its heels were gradually galloping
back   over me the only enemy I know   the barren azure
spreads   when the thing that strips me of everything   that
azure heaven that went on stripping me as I was on the run
shooting from the hip   but even in loving fails once only
and   for good   that moment is the death of me   now I no
longer lack anything now for the first time I am unafraid of
the azure vault   I do not dread that hush nor that infinite
azure for now I shall be undertaken by the earth   now I can
go back to the place where the azure cannot frame his arm
where I need not shoot it out any longer   now my shout will
be answered   now the crack of my rifle will go on echoing
in my ears   now when I can neither hear nor shoot I tried to define
people and find myself in the act of killing   my callow kind
of rule of thumb was garnished with the dyes of blood   but
with blood of others I could not paint out the azure   I
craved my own blood   today I made it I saw to it that my

own blood blackened the azure dome then returned to earth
and now I no longer see nor remember the azure vault   I
smell the smell of my earth and wait for when I shall return
to earth   above me the wind streams I no longer envy the
wind   before long I shall become the wind   before long I
shall live in the azure dome unaware of the azure dome   I
shall turn into a star   a star acquainted with every midnight
every high noon   that keeps on turning around and around.

*Kiss**

When I close my eyes the world withdraws
Only the gravity of tenderness can reassure me . . .
Silence dwindling into the stillness of the night
Circles around us like a promise
It now   becomes an affectionate zone enclosing us
Rather than estranging us
But we suddenly are aware   it is as if we are on our own . . .

We search for each other
In ways more sure than talking or seeing
And we find
When we have lost ourselves —

What was it I desired to make certain of
O tenderness returned from afar
Within this distilled stillness   beyond speech
You are now   only panting for breath

You yourself are   this instant   very life . . .
But soon even these words will be chastened
When gentleness overflows the world
And I drop back to life in it

*Title in English

235   TANIKAWA SHUNTARŌ

Journey 1

A beautiful viewcard
Nothing to write about
I am now   here

Iced coffee is delicious
Strawberry shortcake is delicious
What was the name of that river flowing through the town
Flowing so smoothly

Here   I am now
Because I actually am here
I just don't feel as if I am here

In my memory
I know but
Now nowhere but here
I am

Journey 2

A gypsy
Yelled rapping on the car window
In a tongue not without meaning
Ostia

Mud walls covered with mud
Dried-up wells
Pine-cones

That place is this place
No other place but this place
The gypsy's place is my place
I am in this place
No chance of escape
Even into the blue of the sky
Man has long since reached out his hand and touched it

Journey 3

To the horizon the road running straight
It's painful not to feel anything
Looking back I saw
From the horizon the road running straight

Whether the landscape was large or small it was hard to say
It fell on my eyes
Just that nothing more

Was it the world was it
Was it I
Still without words

But already I find
To reach the wordless centre
Where I am an object of no consequence
My words stand in the way

Journey 4

I look at a picture postcard
Not a memory
Nor the present
Moment

Mind is transparent
Beyond mind the sea is seen
Neither dark nor dazzling

Don't stand in the way
Words
Between me and the sea!

On my temple
A bead of sweat
What illumination
In the place's name

IWATA HIROSHI
(b.1932)

Here In Our Country

(to Picasso)

A golden cock
upon a crown of rock
overlooking a spring.
The grass beside it beds
a King and a Queen kissing,
which enrages the cock,
splits the rock, makes the castle fall,
the castle of Granada.
    Here in our country, we exile *oiran*
    to the river, tied on wooden shutters.

An ox head,
a man with the head of an ox
stabs a dagger on some festival day.
It's you who die with bloody throat,
you with the curly hair, not the chestnut horse,
under the sun, under the sun of night,
buried in scorching sand.
    Here in our country we exile *oiran*
    to the river, tied on wooden shutters.

Ah, a brazen trumpet.
A woman blows an oboe loudly
at an indifferent heaven,
horrified eyes of drops, mouth a bow,
quiet like a clock, propped on one breast
beside men bearing a desert on their backs
    Here in our country we exile *oiran*
    to the river, tied on wooden shutters.

A pigeon on a man's forehead
observes the teeth and cheeks
of a terrified child,
a chair behind him, and fire,
a stone statue in the fire, the statue and a banner,
the banner rips, the chair blazes, the pigeon talks.
   Here in our country we exile *oiran*
   to the river, tied on wooden shutters.

oiran: high-class geisha of the Edo period.

To a Girl

Let my words change into a hand
A very manly hand
Slightly sweaty a little rough
An unromantic hand
Because I must
Thrust my words
Upon you
A girl who has resolved to kill herself
Because that's my privilege
Your duty is
To brood over it again and again
As if running and
Chasing and being chased
Because night is longer than war
Both the government and you are completely alone
There's absolutely no time as painful as morning
Brooding on it hundreds and thousands of times over
And then to plunge to the depths of despair
You intend to swallow two hundred sleeping pills
But the truth is
I want to stuff every hole in your body
With words that taste far worse than pills
Sadists are
Clapping their hands
Let me offer you
My hand!

Not Married Yet

Work work
Heavy work and light work
Finishing works of various colours
I make a telephone call to you
Work work
Blue work and red work
Finishing works with various smells
You wait for my telephone call
Work work work is finished!
Rendezvous at our usual bar
We drink our usual drinks
You a little I a lot
Drinking our usual drinks
We talk of the day's happenings of our work
Of people of tomorrow's plans
And suddenly
In the darkness a kiss
When shall we meet when shall we meet again
Monday Tuesday Wednesday
Thursday Friday Saturday
Mon Tues Wed Thurs Fri Sat!
To your room on Sunday
I go on Sunday
Under the sun of Sundays
We peel our tangerines
How about buying a plot of land on Mars
Shall we hold a horse-race there
Do you think there's any horses on Mars
You don't bother me
Nor interfere with my work
I don't bother you
Nor interfere with your work

243   IWATA HIROSHI

That's why we're happy when we meet
My course is fixed
Your pace never alters
Like the ticking of an invisible clock in the darkness
Then suddenly
Putting on a serious expression you asked me
"Well what's going to become of us now
And
What are we going to do about us
From now on"

Unreasonable young woman useless wheat
Convention-bound sea-waved seaweed
As the sea is deep and dark
Neither our direction nor the course of our work
Can be seen in the deep green
Mon Tues Wed Thurs Fri Sat
Do you think there's any horses on Mars
Such a colour such a weight such a smell!
Seeing clearly the invisible future
The two of us are suddenly frightened

The Extinction of the Animals

Deep in the blue sky
One dazzlingly shiny plane
Then a siren sounded oo-oo-oo-oo-oo-oo-oo
Men murdered beasts in hot haste
Then men were murdered by beasts
Compassionately and painstakingly

This happened just eighteen years ago

Bears died after eating snacks
In the snacks was strychnine nitrate
They died with full stomachs

> Goodbye to dirty drinking-water and armfuls of straw
> Eating in coaxed confinement
> Such was my life

Lions died after taking breakfast
In their breakfast was strychnine nitrate
They died with full stomachs

> Goodbye to dirty drinking-water and armfuls of straw
> Eating in coaxed confinement
> Such was my life

The elephants didn't eat anything
Thirty days forty days
They died with empty stomachs

> Goodbye to dirty drinking-water and armfuls of straw.

245   IWATA HIROSHI

Tigers died after having their dinners
In the dinners was strychnine nitrate
They died with full stomachs

    Goodbye to dirty drinking-water and . . . .

Pythons died after a bedtime snack
In the bedtime snack was strychnine nitrate
They died with full stomachs

    Goodbye to dirty . . . .

This happened just eighteen years ago

Compassionately and painstakingly
Before men were murdered by beasts
Men murdered beasts in hot haste
Then a siren sounded oo-oo-oo-oo-oo-oo-oo
One dazzlingly shiny plane
Flew deep into the blue sky

KŌRA RUMIKO
(b.1932)

Jewellery Counter

Life effervesces but we cannot penetrate the gems
this is a place where a tongue not ours predominates
and certain human shadows thinner than paper
superimpose themselves on one another there.

Young girls approach here like copper coins incising light
and letting fall their shadows on the plate glass
extend their weightless arms across the jewels
which hold themselves aloof creating whorls of air around them.

When under the supple light cast here
the stones present their faces to the girls
what evil in them can it be that always burns with brilliant grace?
And what can be the nothingness irradiating chasmed silences
            within their hearts?

Falling languidly upon themselves   they lie
self-contained as noh masks   upon the brows of former faces
where the past goes on eating time incessantly away
not leaving any wound unhealed upon the surface of the earth.

When within their glittering confines
inevitable tomorrow seizes the whole of me
they no longer will preserve that brilliance that illusion
and like a veil of white petals will be whirled away across the
            cracked horizon.

Encounter

I miss my footing on the stairs,
and find myself in front of a door
which I open and see you there.

> (I don't need you, so
> I'd just as soon you vanished.)

Turned into a sharp knife, I
run through the town.

The air, like a balloon, comes
billowing towards me.
Wriggling among the staring eyes, I
stab the folds of air and the
invisible walls of words.

Tomorrow,
another person who is myself and not myself
will exchange friendly greetings with you,
who will have missed your footing on the stairs and
broken open the door.

Contemplation

I hear a hundred voices mutter and complain
behind my back

I hear a thousand voices mutter and complain
away ahead of me

I don't know how to still the thousand voices any more than
      the hundred voices —
I dissipate the voices in my own way

I select products painted with plastic that is their sweat
and sell them these   under an agreement with the military
(their motors function without thinking)

Without me people might get along better
but my own way works as well as their's
without me people might get along better
but after all here am I

and so what matters is what I think —
without me
nothing would get done in the end
without me
there would be no progress and no happiness.

A Tree

In a tree, there is
a tree still not in existence,
whose crest is even now
trembling in some breeze.

In a blue sky, there is
a blue sky still not in existence,
whose horizon is now being
pierced by a swift bird.

In a body, there is
a body still not in existence,
whose altar is now being
flooded with fresh blood.

In a town, there is
a town still not in existence,
whose main square is now being
swung in my direction.

Awake

After things have been crowding against one another
and passing across me
and trees silently turn the backs of their leaves
and take the world away from me.

Out of this void I extend a hand
and touch the cheek of wood's hot grain
a naked arm and
beneath the earth   circling round and round
the dark rocks.

    (I escaped from futility
    I followed the curves of the leaves of darkness
    towards the boundary beyond
    because you were there
    because you were not there.)

    In the furnace fired by matter of various kinds
    the eyes under their closed lids
    seek speeds faster than the speed of dust falling at dawn.

Translucent morning light
has opened my eyelids from within
and a crisis has just awakened.
My hand mixes the unknown breath of things
with the unseen mornings of the earth.

YOSHIHARA SACHIKO
(b.1932)

Madness

Eyes shut tight
I hear my brains go splat and scatter
like dry tea-leaves.

I must kill
one lovely languid serpent after another.

A horse lies dangling upside down   and a moon rising
Mary with a child in her arms   weeps with red eyes —
now watch me whittle my finger away
and paint red characters.

One streak of white hair   many streaks of white hair
I am not to blame   it's the dreams the paper that are to blame.

A car crashes into another car   slowly   undersea.
Whittling my finger   sharpening it like a pencil
let me write in red   O Mary   what words do you want me to
        write down?

Darkness comes rushing on me   with waves   with fever
a knife comes flying to me   with a cat   O burst the window!

Pitiful
O everything   each and everyone so pitiful.

Flowers

In springtime when I was young
the sun kept smiling its shining smile
where cherry flowers were blooming at the full —

lively husks of earth
airy scales flaking away   blown by a breeze
the petals whirling settle and die one by one
each one stained with translucent blood —

and just like that white cotton thread stitching a wound
a line of flashes
piercing and piecing together each rag of time
that withers away perpetually —
a pale-faced machine all on its own
goes on stitching together pages of *pensees*.

sensation!

Let me shed tears and play with garlands of flowers
ah my perished hours —

but   among all these cherry flowers
the evening is about to drown

leaving a faint haze
of shredded white cotton thread.

Fever

Evening dusky
vast translucent snail of dew

comes creeping from a corner of the yard —

crushed   the snail of dew
has such a weight

its smoke-tinged life
has such a weight.

The dagger of mercury thrust into my armpit
gives me such icy pain

I am so utterly tired today
I am tired of grieving any more —

blue scum on the pool of castor-oil
a red moon on the needles of castor-oil plants —

I drown   I am drowning
I feel sad about my life.

What is this fragrance?

High up in the maidenhair tree
my home-made anemoscope is bickering round and round.

Anaemia

My feet on the ground

suddenly all around me spreads
a white sea of sunlight
        (cicadas shrilling in hot summer)

I see some crippled beast (what is it?)
crawling across the white yard
dark eyes smiling
in a patch of shade

I have nothing
I have nothing but those dark eyes
I have nothing but this white sunshine

in the flooding noon
I smell white blood
        (cicadas still shrilling in hot summer).

Kitchen Table

There is something I musn't do
though I don't know why

when I sit patiently in the half-dark of the room
I feel a blue draught blowing through   bringing *angst* —

there are   nevertheless   many tender-hearted things

asparagus   some stalks thick   some thin
a dish of crab salad with a tiny insect landed in it
a mad woodcutter singing some song on the mountain
          behind my house.

I know I am not alone any longer   and yet
I sometimes feel this heavy sadness

— dusk
I feel it sad and heavy upon me.

Name

Yes, one day
one day
it shall be revealed that

snow is not flowers,
seas are not skies,

 wind does not sing,
 donkeys are not horses,
 and fathers are not our mothers' lovers —

But I shall go on
wrongly calling
wind light,
clouds roses,
you my love,
just as I have always done.

Good things are all the same, and
beautiful things cannot be mistaken.

If one thing exists in all, and
all things exist in one,
we must call them all by the same name —

Appetite

Starvation is
the sin born within me.
Why is there so little of it
in this grey, stolid building?

Starvation is
the punishment I was given.
Now it too must be punished for seeking
seeking what there is so little of.

All the same, unfortunately,
I dislike overeating, and
whatever I eat seems to poison me.

Nevertheless, I am always ready to eat
what I am and what I am not —
autumn, love, a glittering airplane, and
time that ebbs and flows outside the window-panes.

Rainbow

From the tram window, how I don't quite know,
I caught a brief vanishing glimpse of a pig eating grass
on the almost vertical slope of a field after a shower.
It was not a cow, nor a goat, nor a hare.
But was it really a pig?

There must be many strange sights
that go unnoticed.
Seeing them, as it were, in false pictures, there must exist
a cock without a crest,
a snake with legs,
a desk without legs,
a man without heart,
love without embraces —

Now I have this dazzling picture before me,
in which I know there is something very wrong,
and yet I can't say what it is however hard I try.

Get lost, rainbow!

Resurrection

To kill love in order not to die   that is self-defence
the pistol pointed at you is pointed at my heart
the flame of crime and the ice of punishment
make me crack open and should I break in two
there will be a hole like a lie   which will probably
silently expand   that is death
the sound of earth dripping   will recede   and then
to be in a cell for a long long time
with its one window where there might perhaps be
unquiet death   burning death   burning life
in the rain a spider weaving a web   wet with his own sweat
reducing and annihilating the shining oblong of O.

NAKAE TOSHIO
(b.1933)

Sounds

Quietly things turn round
With an interrogatory "Who?"
Already running into gloom
Holding both hands in front of it.

At such moments
We find ourselves unable to grasp this world of ours
We two touch one another's hearts
Involuntarily asking
"What shall we do?"
And laugh hesitantly.

Night and Fish

Fish at night
Feel themselves flowing
Out of the ground
As there is less water
Waving their tails and fins faster
As the night is too quiet
They are nervous about their splashing
Afraid the sound may disturb someone
They peep into the night
And
See a water-boatman
Spinning round and round
As if it had lost is way back and forgotten to brood over it.

About Loneliness

Don't gaze at one bird in a wood
For it's one with those far away
No matter how alone it may be

Don't look at one fish
For it'll never talk
To any other fish
In the stream

Don't keep brooding on one thing
Night falls while you are pondering
Then you'll be unable to talk about the night and break down

When you look at something that isn't there
There's something that tells you falteringly
About something that is there

The one within you but whom you ignore
Forgets at such moments to go home
Like a lone bird in a wood.

TOMIOKA TAEKO
(b.1935)

The Story of Myself

Father, mother, midwife and
All the prophets foretold that
I should be a boy; that's why
I had to break the placenta to be born
As a girl.

Then they were all so sorry; that's why
I made myself into a boy.
Then they all admired me; that's why
I made myself into a girl.
Then they all started picking on me; that's why
I made myself into a boy.

In my late teens,
I found a boy for my lover; that's why
I reluctantly made myself into a girl again.
Then, all of them except my lover said
I had become a girl; that's why
I made myself a boy for all except my lover.
But I began to resent being a girl even for my lover; that's why
I made myself into a boy. Then he refused to go to bed with me;
That's why I made myself into a girl.

Meanwhile several centuries had passed.
Now the poor had started a bloody revolution
Only to find themselves subdued for a piece of bread.
That's why I became a medieval church; calling
My wares of love, I delivered old clothes and rice balls
From door to door.

Meanwhile several centuries had passed.
Now the Kingdom of God had come to pass, and
The rich and the poor had become great friends.

That's why I scattered incendiary leaflets
From my private helicopter.

Meanwhile several centuries had passed.
Now the bloody revolutionaries were kneeling
Before a rusty cross.
I saw the flame of the cosmos in chaos.
That's why
I, in the tavern of a cell, spend hours and hours
With Byron, Musset,
Villon, Baudelaire,
Hemingway and girls in black trousers, playing cards, drinking,
Arguing with serious passion about what bohemianism is here in
      Japan,
Arguing and arguing about what we call love at first sight,
Making fun of one another.

Father, mother, midwife and
All called me a wonder child; that's why
I became a feeble-minded child.
They called me an idiot; that's why
I became an intellectual and built my home out of sight.
I had more physical strength than I knew what to do with.

When I became famous as an out-of-sight intellectual
I began to step out
Along the footpath.
It was the footpath of father and mother.
Now the devil of perversity was embarrassed.
The devil of perversity was in agony with its honour at stake.
That's why
I made myself into a fine girl,
Making myself into a boy for my lover,
And keeping him forever without complaint.

265   TOMIOKA TAEKO

*Between**

There are two kinds of sorrow we might as well be proud of:

When at the start of the day
Slamming the room door behind me,
slamming the house door behind me,
I stand on the street invisible in the rain of the rainy season,
I wonder how I shall spend my day,
I wonder what I shall do today.
I find I am neither for nor against either side.
To whom shall I speak about these concrete questions I want to ask
I, a hater of war, but not a pacifist,
Am filled with sorrow that all I can do is just
To keep on trying to keep my eyes open.

There are two kinds of sorrow we might as well be proud of:

I, though together with you,
Cannot understand what you are;
That's how I know you are there,
That's how I know I am here.
I am filled with sorrow that I cannot understand you,
I am filled with sorrow that you are no one but yourself.

*Title in English

TAKAHASHI MUTSUO
(b.1937)

The Finger

Swathed in
Many and
Many a petal
Slumbers my dawn

Some day from that gloomy heaven blanketed in cloud
A single candid finger will emerge
And spurt forth
Discovering my rosy morn

My jumping soul
That had been sealed away
Will overflow the space between the heavens and earth
With resounding echoes

In filthy garments, deep in sordid night
I am dreaming in rapture
Morning will come
Like the grace of bread

The finger stirs now
In the oceanic chaos
Of distant daybreak.

Portrait of Myself at the Start

A young man squats to fasten his shoelaces
How delicate the nape of his neck looks
The flesh on his shoulders that moves slowly and softly
And the two thighs projecting from his loins are young and round
(The male nipple pressed hard between his thighs is still pale pink)
The clean straight eyes of a silent young beast
Are fastened to the fingers fastening the shoelaces
But the moving fingers are dreaming absorbedly
Of the region a little above them
Of the bottle to his belly that is as lithe as a hungry wolf's
There where they would play with gentle Eros cased in his thin skin
And who now dozes in his lustrous tender grasses
The youth stands up and starts to walk stark naked
But for his laced-up boots
He keeps on walking and then grows old
An old man hardening his face never looking back
But behind the old man the youth often crouches to fasten his
        shoelaces
And then stands up again and begins to walk
For the nth time.

Portrait of Myself as an Ancient Goddess

Young man standing in the stone-paved square of this castle town
You whose rustic origins are revealed
In your bare feet that do not wear even sandals
Look up above the worn-out stone steps ascending before you
Look upon this dreadful visage I have as I stand entire in the Temple
You who stand a simple sundial standing exactly at right-angles
       to the ground
You are dragging not only your own summer morning shadow
You are dragging along behind you the scent of soil
The fragrance of vegetation the tang of water the smell of cowpats
       in the fields
I like those innocent startled shiny eyes with which you gaze upon me
I like the young fragrant darkness of your wide open mouth
My love has to devour all your terror your ignorance your whole
       youthfulness
My mouth that stretches from ear to ear must kiss yours
The crimson of my cheeks must be stained anew with your crimson
       blood
For I shall drain you dry starting with the lips on which I now
       press mine
Come young man you cannot escape me now that you have cast
       your eyes upon me
Behind our blood-smeared wedding
The whole world shall go up in flames like the legendary city
       of sin
Existence is always going up in flames just so.

Portrait of Myself as a Baby-killer

Shall I give you the true reasons why I have to kill babies
because a thousand newborn babies will one day be a
    thousand powerful kings
because I am in reality a humble beggar surrounded by a
    thousand kings
because the beggar must defend the throne and the throne
    must be kept apart
because the lonely sword must always be wet with the
    blood of kings
because the lonely beggar must be guarded by ghosts of the
    slaughtered kings
because my throne must receive the praises of the grief-
    stricken and cursing mothers of kings
Retainers and soldiers are alarmed and terrified but they do
    not know who I am
At midnight I rise from my throne and dragging my heavy
    gangrenous feet
Mount to the top of the palace observation tower the highest
    point in the kingdom
I gaze out upon the extent of that region reigned over by the
    beggar
Beyond the undulating plain that is still and soundless as
    death itself
A thousand kings will be born when the tide is full in the
    invisible sea
And my soldiers will run lifting their swords in their hands
Through the restless darkness the dawning darkness of my
    realm
I shall add a thousand grey hairs to my hair
I take a heavy breath and descend the steps
Grey hairs grow thickly there even on the treads.

Portrait of Myself in the Final Fire

Not the flames ascending a tower of wood piled in parallel
      crosses
But perfunctory flames issuing from gas jets will scorch me
Tears will stream and my whole body will crackle
But I will not rise up like an ancient monarch
For the prosaic flames from the gas jets are unworthy of such
      an act
Nevertheless myself at the age of a hundred . . . myself at
      fifty . . . myself at thirty-seven
Myself at ten . . . and at one year . . . all will crackle at once
And all of my crackling selves burst into tears all at once
Then to be rent and split into milliards of the minutest
      fragments in the world
The milliards of fragmented particles will share my self with
      one another
If an unknown fire has created my self out of milliards of
      particles a long while ago
By mixing them up and synthesizing them into my self
Then the banal flames of the gas jets that burn my self may
      be mysterious fire too
For when that mysterious fire was creating my self
I must have had beautiful tears in my eyes.

271   TAKAHASHI MUTSUO

IKEDA SOME
(b.c.1875)

Umeboshi

---

*An old woman of ninety remembers the explosion of the A-bomb at
Hiroshima*

Well, that time . . . let me see,
I fell over with the cupboard in the living-room.

The house shook and shook and shook and
I crawled out onto the roof
I did not crawl out of my own accord, naturally
I should rather say "I was made to do it
By God or by Buddha."

O, what misery.
O, what pain.
I wanted the breath to be taken from my body
And to go to heaven.

It was on the third morning after the explosion
Someone put an *umeboshi* in my mouth.

"This old woman is dead," they said. "What a shame!"
They prayed the Buddhist prayer: *"Namu-amida, namu-amida."*

"I am alive. I am alive," I told them.
They put a big *umeboshi* in my mouth.

Umeboshi's nice and tasty, you know
I must express my thanks to the *umeboshi*, because
I soon got well again.

umeboshi: a pickled Japanese plum, a cheap and common delicacy.

SUYAMA HISAYO
(b.1882)

Arranging Flowers

When not myself
I arrange flowers:
    a horse-tail grass
    two begonias
    ancient twigs
released from everything
untroubled by anything
until I meet myself again.

Haiku

Rose mallow in full bloom
smiling to herself
and falling tomorrow.

My Hands

Looking at my own hands
I cannot help saying thank you to them
for the many years of hard work
they took on for me.

Once I presented one of my bony fingers with a ring
Only to find it did not become me;
It could never warm my heart . . .

O let me go on living as before,
with no ornament but this simplicity
which I believe is my only pride.

275   SUYAMA HISAYO

The Stream

Rushing
   and dashing
and rolling in torrents
   pounding the falls
washing the rocks
   swirling the leaves
whispering here
   crying out there
the stream goes down to a wide wide ocean.

The long voyage of water
like a human life.
— I feel like crying out
          crying out

Wind

Tree leaves — where are they going, scuffling
Along the endless road,
Dragging their dry crackling steps
Driven onwards by the gales of wind?

Despite the breath of spring
The chill sound strikes at
The secret heart of earth, that is breaking, but
Obstinately refuses to give a sign of life.

In swirling wind, black raindrops vainly
Catch at the old throat with dry coughings
Till trembling water-splashes weep in darkness.

Driven by the gale, they keep shuffling
Feeble feet along the earth in the drenched dark,
Keep playing their eerie tune in
Endless whirlpools of vexed anxiety.

NISHIO KATSUKO
(b.1923)

At a Cannery

The white eyes of the red-faced crabs are glaring at
the noisy women all around them.
Day after day is a black day for crabs at the cannery.
Upon the soft bed of the conveyor-belt, they cry:
"Hey, tell me, what have they done with my hands and feet?"
"Hey, tell me, what have they done with my insides?"

But the women, pretending not to hear anything, work on,
their hands busy and tireless.

Then the white glaring eyes are thrown into a tub.
not even allowed to say goodbye to one another.
The processed bits of crabs are sealed into the pitch blackness
        of cans
but go on cyring:
"Hey, help me out! I want to go home!"

But the women are set-faced, working away on the torrent dashing
along the conveyor-belt, as if all they have to live for
is to despatch crabs to the tables of cultivated gentlemen.

ITŌ MARIKO
(b.1939)

The Ladder

We believed we were climbing the ladder of industry
to reach the goal of peace and happiness.

Higher and higher we climbed, as they climbed the Tower
of Babel,
as Jack climbed the beanstalk, the ladder of our
desires . . .

But one day, the Devil's lightning-flash burnt down
the ladder.
though not our desire to rise to peace and happiness.

And so today, hundreds of thousands of ghosts are still
whirling like winds, longing to reach an understanding

through the spaces of our strange times.

YOSHIYUKI RIE
(b.1939)

Carrying

A bird soars upwards.
A boy, suddenly snatched up in its beak, is being
carried up to the peak of a youthful dream, soon
to be broken by a shot silenced in darkness.

Soon you will be hearing those light footsteps
carrying another morning. Fallen leaves are being
dragged along the pavements as black time
is broken to pieces against the wind.

Carrying on my back a dreaming baby
whose tender head is hugged in a woolly hat, I
am crossing a rustic bridge supported only by
my own thin arms.

NOMA FUMIYO
(b.c.1945)

The Real Meaning

It was always so.
The girl whose life was blasted by the atom bomb
Has never known the real meaning of health.

On that day, when she was still only a baby
The hand of death was laid upon her,
Barring her forever from the real meaning of happiness.

Every year we give these pretentious speeches about
No more Hiroshimas, under dry summer skies all white
With doves. — But O, the real meaning of peace
Could never disintegrate like this
To the sounds of war still shaking the earth.

MATSUSHIMA MAMI

In a Poor Hamlet

In a lonely hamlet in Tōhoku, two little children died.
They died of hunger and cold.

What was I doing as they died?
What were you doing then?

Lovers sitting on a small bench
Were playing their little games of love.
Families kept holding on to their little worlds
Within the four corners of their little homes.

I was slurping noodles with my feet on the foot-warmer.

O why can't we remove all these petty screens around us,
And let our love flow outwards, ever wider, wider,
Until the whole world becomes one wonderful family?

Those little children died there all alone.

Anonymous

Chewing Gum

Teacher, don't scold me.
Teacher, don't scold me, please.
I did a very wrong thing.
I stole a piece of chewing-gum from a store.
I did it with a younger girl.

Immediately they found out what we had done.
Perhaps God told them.
I could not say anything.
I was shaking like a clockwork toy.
I told the younger girl to steal it.
She said: "You take one as well."
But I said "No" as I was afraid to be found out.

So she did it.
But it is I who am wrong.
I am a thousand and ten thousand times
More wrong than she is.
It is I who did wrong.

I had thought that what we did
Would not get to the ears of my mother.
But she soon found out all about it.
I have never seen such a dreadful look
As the one she gave me then.
I have never seen such a mournful look
As the one she gave me then.

I was thumped so hard I thought I was going to die.
"A child such as this cannot be ours. Get out of this house,"
She shouted, weeping.

I went out on my own.
I went to a park where I frequently walk.
But teacher, I felt as if I were in a foreign land.
I thought to myself, I must go somewhere,
I must go — but there was no place to go.

I thought and thought about it.
But I could not get a single thing clear in my mind,
And my legs were trembling.

I went home very late that evening,
And bowed flat as a fish before my mother, apologizing.
But she just went on weeping, staring me in the face.
Why did I do such a bad thing?

— Since then two days have passed.
My mother is still weeping mournfully.
What shall I do, teacher?
What shall I do?

By an anonymous Japanese schoolgirl.

Biographical Notes
by A. R. Davis

Aida Tsunao was born on 17 March 1914 in the Honjo ward of Tokyo. He failed to complete his course in the Department of Sociology in Nihon University. In 1940 he volunteered for military service and was posted to China. While in Nanking he became friendly with Kusano Shinpei and contributed poems to the magazines *Kōchō* (Oriole; published in Nanking) and *Ajia* (Asia, published in Shanghai), with which Kusano was associated. After the war he became a member of Kusano's revived *Rekitei* group. His first collection, *Kanko* (Salt Lake, 1957), received the first Takamura Kōtarō Prize in 1958.

Aota Mitsuko was born in 1907 in Nara prefecture, where she graduated from the Takada Girls' High School. She contributed to *Jikan* (Time) in its first period (1930–31) after earlier being a member of the *Nihon Shidan* (Japan Poetry Circle, first series 1925–30) group. Currently she is a member of the Japan Women Poets Association.

Ayukawa Nobuo was born in August 1920 in Tokyo. He attended the Waseda Middle School and the Waseda First Senior High School and afterwards entered the English Literature course at Waseda University but left without graduating in 1942. He was called up and saw service in Sumatra, from where he was invalided home to Japan in 1944. He had begun to establish himself as an *avant-garde* poet from 1937 when he contributed to Nakagiri Masao's *Luna* and Murano Shirō's *Shin-ryōdo*. He brought into being the first *Arechi* (Waste Land), which ran for six numbers (1939–41). After the war he was a central figure in the group that founded the second *Arechi* magazine (1947–48) and produced the six *Arechi* anthologies (1951–58). He published a *Poetical Works* in 1955 and a *Complete Poetical Works* in 1965. He is also known for his studies *Gendaishi Sakuhō* (The Composition of Modern Poetry, 1955) and *Ayukawa Nobuo Shiron-shū* (A.N.'s Essays on Poetry, 1965) and has translated T.S. Eliot's *The Use of Poetry and the Use of Criticism* (1954).

Hagiwara Sakutarō (1 November 1886–11 May 1942). The eldest son of a doctor in Maebashi, Gunma prefecture, north-west of Tokyo, at that time a major centre of silk manufacture. Hagiwara gained recognition as a poet from his middle school days when he had three *tanka* published in *Myōjō* (1903). His parents and teachers found him lazy. After graduating late from the Maebashi Middle School, he successively entered the Fifth Higher School in Kumamoto (1907), the Sixth in Okayama (1908) and the preparatory course at Keiō University (1911) but in each case failed to make progress. He turned for a while to the opera and the new spoken drama and began to learn the mandolin (music remained important throughout his life). In 1912 he began to write *shi* under the influence of Kitahara Hakushū's *Omoide*. Hakushū's *Zanboa* (Pomelo) published five lyrics by him in 1913, and the same year saw the beginning of his friendship with Murō Saisei. The two later founded the magazine *Kanjō* (Feelings). Hagiwara's first collection *Tsuki ni Hoeru* (Baying the Moon, 1917), first printed at his own expense, was immediately recognized to have changed existing concepts and to have established a modern lyricism in contemporary language. His solitary and world-weary feelings, following his increasing neurasthenia and heavy drinking, grew more and more desperate in his later volumes, but to his death he remained a power in modern poetry. He was one of the founders of the *Shiki* (Four Seasons) school of the 1930s. Besides his poetry he wrote many critical works of which the best known is *Shi no Genri* (The Principles of Poetry, 1928).

Hasegawa Ryūsei was born on 19 June 1928 in Senba, Ōsaka. He studied French Literature at Waseda University but did not graduate. He became a member of the *Rettō* (Archipelago) group of socialist realist poets of the first half of the 1950s. His first collection *Paorō no Tsuru* (The Cranes of Paolo) was published in 1957 and was followed by *Tora* (Tiger) in 1960 and a *Complete Poetical Works* in 1967. Hasegawa has stressed the narrative and dramatic aims of his poetry and always acknowledges the influence of Ono Tōzaburō. He works as the head of the development centre of a Tokyo advertising agency.

Hino Sōjō (18 July 1901–29 January 1956). Born in the Shitaya ward of Tokyo, he grew up in Korea, where his father worked for the Seoul–Pusan Railway. He returned to attend the Third Higher School in Kyoto in 1918. After graduating in 1921, he studied law at Kyoto Imperial University (1921–24) and then joined the Ōsaka Marine Fire Insurance Company (he moved to the Sumitomo Marine Fire Insurance Company in 1944). Sōjō, who had begun writing *haiku* under his father's guidance while still a schoolboy, became a leading figure in the emerging New Haiku movement from the time he founded the Kyoto University Third Higher School Haiku Society and launched the magazine *Kyō-ganoko* (Kyoto Fawn) in 1920. *Kyō-ganoko* was short-lived, but later he joined in founding *Kikan* (Flagship) and editing it for five years (1935–40). He published his first *haiku* collection, *Hana-gōri* (Flower Ice), in 1927.

Horiguchi Daigaku was born on 8 January 1892 in the Hongō ward of Tokyo, virtually at the gate of the Imperial University, where his father was then a law student. Hence his given name Daigaku (university). He grew up in Nagaoka, Niigata prefecture, in the care of his grandmother. She brought him to Tokyo in 1909, when he joined the New Poetry Society. He entered the preparatory course at Keiō University in the next year with Satō Haruo, who became a life-long friend. In 1911 he withdrew to accompany his diplomat father to Mexico. He began to study French and was introduced by his father to the Parnassians. In 1913 he went with his father to Europe, where he studied symbolist poetry. He spent most of the next twelve years abroad in Europe and in Brazil. In this time he established himself as a leading translator and introducer of French literature and published his first three volumes of poems. His anthology of translations of contemporary French poetry, *Gekka no Ichigun* (A Herd in the Moonlight, 1925), exerted a great influence on early Shōwa poetry, just as his translation of Paul Morand's *Ouvert la nuit* in 1924 contributed profoundly to the style of the Shin-kankaku-ha (New Sense School) of fiction-writers. His achievement as a translator (some 140 volumes) has overshadowed his poetry, but he has published more than twenty collections.

Horikawa Masami was born on 17 February 1931 in Hatagaya, Tokyo. He failed to complete his course in Russian Literature at Waseda University. He had begun to write poetry in about 1949, and in 1954 he joined with others to found the magazine *Han* (Overflowing), which lasted until August 1959. From 1961 until its demise in September 1964 he was a member of the editorial committee of the important *Gendaishi* (Modern Poetry). Subsequently he became editor of *Gendaishi Techō* (Modern Poetry Notebook). He published his collection *Taiheiyō* (The Pacific) in 1964.

Ibaragi Noriko (*née* Miura Noriko) was born on 12 June 1926 in Jusō, Ōsaka. She graduated from the Imperial Women's College of Pharmacy. In 1953 she joined with Kawasaki Hiroshi (b. 1930), Tanikawa Shuntarō, and others in founding the important magazine *Kai* (Oar). With her collections *Taiwa* (Conversation, 1955), *Mienai Haitatsu-fu* (Invisible Postmen, 1958), and *Chinkon-ka* (Requiems, 1965) she has become one of the established women poets. Because her work has escaped the general pessimism of her generation, it has attracted descriptions such as "healthy", "civic", "well-intentioned". She is also the author of a book of biographies of poets for children and a number of radio plays.

Ikeda Some is described by the editor of the anthology in which her *"Umeboshi"* appears as a woman of ninety who wrote the poem in remembrance of her experiences at the time of the atom bomb upon Hiroshima. No other information is available.

Irizawa Yasuo was born on 3 November 1931 in Matsue, Shimane prefecture, on the west coast of the main island of Japan. In his student days at the University of Tokyo, where he obtained a master's degree in French Language and Literature, he contributed to the poetry magazine *Bokutachi no Mirai no tame ni* (For Our Future). When this ceased publication, he joined with other of the former contributors in founding *Amorphe*. He subsequently became a member of the *Rekitei* group. After working for the publishers Chikuma Shobō on graduation for a year and a half, he became an associate professor of French Language and Literature at Meiji Gakuin. He resigned from this post in

1969. The first of his several volumes of poems, *Shiawase soretomo Fushiawase* (Good Luck or Ill Luck), appeared in 1955. He has also published *Shi no Kōzō ni tsuite no Oboegaki* (Notes on Poetic Structure, 1968) and translations of Gérard de Nerval.

Ishigaki Rin was born on 21 February 1920 in the fashionable Akasaka quarter of Tokyo, where she completed higher primary school. She began writing poetry in the pre-war period as a member of the *Dansō* group of women writers (the magazine *Dansō* ran from June 1939 to November 1940) and took Fukuda Masao (1893–1952) as her model. After the war she followed Itō Shinkichi (b. 1906) and eventually joined the *Rekitei* group. Her first volume of poems, *Watakushi no mae ni aru Nabe to O-kama to Moeru Hi to* (The Pot, the Kettle and the Blazing Fire in Front of Me), appeared in 1959. After her second volume, *Hyōsatsu nado* (Nameplate, etc., 1968), she was awarded the Mr H. Prize for 1969. In 1975 she retired from the Nihon Kōgyō Bank, for which she had worked for many years.

Ishikawa Takuboku was born, according to the family register, on 20 February 1886 (it has been held that he was actually born in October or December 1885) in a Zen temple of the Sōtō sect, of which his father Ittei was the chief monk, in Hinoto village, Iwate prefecture, in northern Japan. He died on 13 April 1912. His formal education ended in October 1902 with his withdrawal from middle school (where his results had conspicuously declined) after a reprimand on suspicion of cheating in an examination, but he had already been drawn to the romantic poetry of Yosano Tekkan and Yosano Akiko and published his first *tanka* in the *Myōjō* number of the same month. The remaining ten years of his life, passed between Tokyo, Hokkaidō, and his home, were filled with difficulties; he worked as a substitute primary school teacher and in a variety of jobs in journalism. Yet he was throughout recognized as a genius, and he received financial and other help from many friends. His first collection of *shi*, *Akogare* (Yearning, May 1905), carried a preface by Ueda Bin and a postface by Yosano Tekkan and enjoyed two printings of a thousand copies. It was a skilful capturing of the current romantic mood, and Takuboku afterwards rejected it. His true successes were his two *tanka* collections, *Ichiaku no*

Suna (A Handful of Sand, December 1910) and *Kanashiki Gangu* (A Pitiful Toy, June 1912), in which he answered the contemporary call for naturalism by a direct and simple self-expression, found also in his *Romaji Diary* and his letters and maintained as the true form of poetry in his critique *Kurōbeki Shi* (Poems to Eat; first serialized in *Mainichi Shinbun*, November 1909). His posthumous collection of *shi*, *Yobiko to Kuchibue* (Piping and Whistling), includes poems which seem to show him moving towards a socialist position. Both the man and his work maintain their appeal in present Japan.

Itō Mariko was born in 1939 in Hiroshima, where she is now a contributor to local poetry magazines.

Iwasa Tōichirō (8 March 1905–31 May 1974). Born in Tokyo, he graduated from the Department of French Literature of Hōsei University. He modelled his poetry on that of Hinatsu Kōnosuke (1890–1971) and Horiguchi Daigaku. During the 1930s he was associated with a number of magazines: the most important was *Bungei Hanron* (Outline of Literature), which he edited for 150 issues from September 1931 until February 1944. His attempt to found a successor after the war under the name *Kindaishi-en* (Garden of Modern Poetry) failed after three issues. The first of his collections, *Promenade*, was published in 1923 and was followed by some six others.

Iwata Hiroshi is the pen-name of Ogasawara Toyoki, born on 3 March 1932 in Hokkaidō. He studied Russian at the Tokyo University of Foreign Studies but did not graduate. He was one of the founders with Yoshioka Minoru, Ōoka Makoto, and others of the magazine *Wani* (Crocodile). Afterwards he joined the editorial committee of *Gendaishi* (Modern Poetry) which ended its ten-year run in September 1964. His first collection, *Dokusai* (Despotism), appeared in 1956; later he published *Iya-na Uta* (Unpleasant Songs, 1959), *Zunō no Sensō* (War of the Brains, 1962), and *Guantanamo* (1964). He is also known as a translator of modern Russian literature under his own name.

Kaneko Mitsuharu (25 December 1895–30 June 1975). Born in Tsushima, Aichi prefecture, in a family named Ōshika, he was adopted by the Kanekos at the age of two. After an unstable and unruly boyhood in which he already showed artistic and literary gifts, he entered the preparatory course in English Literature at Waseda in 1913. He withdrew in the following year to enter the Tokyo Art School but hardly attended before he transferred in the autumn to Keiō. Here again he withdrew after a year, but from this year (1916) his interest in poetry began. His first collection, published at his own expense (1919), went unnoticed, and in the same year he left for Europe, going first to London and then to Belgium. Here he lived in a Brussels suburb and read Verhaeren, Samain, Régnier, and Baudelaire. Afterwards he spent some time in Paris. His collection *Kogane-mushi* (Gold Bug, 1923), the product of his two years in Europe, was highly acclaimed. In 1924 he married Mori Michiyo, then a student but who was also to publish poetry. They were extremely poor, and when they set out for France in 1929 they were to spend two of the four years they were away on the outward and return journey, for they had to find their travel expenses *en route* by whatever means they could. For Kaneko life in Japan was oppressive, and his collection *Same* (Shark), published as a book in 1937, contains veiled anti-war, anti-nationalist poems. He continued to write throughout the war years independent and critical poems which were published in his early post-war collections. The post-war period was one of sustained activity by the ageing poet. Besides a dozen volumes of poems (*Ningen no Higeki*, the Tragedy of Man, 1952, received the Yomiuri Prize for Literature), he wrote his auto-biography, *Shijin* (Poet, 1957), and essays on Japanese art and society. His poetry has a savage quality—"nihilistic" is the usual critical epithet—but with an underlying deep humanity.

Kihara Kōichi was born on 13 February 1922 in Hachiōji, Tokyo. He completed the course in building construction at the Tokyo Prefectural School of Technology and during the war served as a construction engineer in China. He had already contributed to Kitasono Katsue's *VOU* in its first period (1935–40), and after the war he again wrote for it and for *Junsui Shi* (Pure Poetry) and *Arechi* (Waste Land). In August 1947 he became an editor with Jō Samon (b. 1904) and Saga

Nobuyuki of *Shigaku* (Poetry Studies). He published *Hoshi no Shōzō* (Portrait of Stars), a collection of prose-poems, in 1954, and followed this with a *Poetical Works* from the Arechi Press two years later. A further collection, *Aru Toki Aru Basho* (Once in a Certain Place), appeared in 1958.

Kinoshita Mokutarō, pen-name of Ōta Masao (1 August 1885–15 October 1945). Born in what is now part of Itō City in Shizuoka prefecture, the youngest of seven children of a wealthy family, he was sent at thirteen to the Deutsche Vereinigung school in Tokyo, where he became friends with Nagata Hideo (1885–1950), like himself to become a member of the Decadent group at the end of Meiji. The literary leanings of both developed at school. Kinoshita's family, however, opposed his wish to study German literature at the university and he was forced to enter the Faculty of Medicine at Tokyo Imperial University in 1906. In the next year he was introduced by Nagata to Yosano Tekkan and became a member of the New Poetry Society and a contributor to *Myōjō*. With Tekkan and Kitahara Hakushū he took part in the *Myōjō* poets' Kyūshū expedition and produced out of it not only poems but plays characterized by *Nanban* (Southern Barbarian) exoticism. Through the period of the Pan Society he was an important figure in modern poetry circles, but medicine, in which he was to achieve distinction, gradually from 1916 on drew him away from the literary world. His collected poems were published in 1930.

Kinoshita Yūji (27 October 1914–4 August 1965). Born in what is now Fukuyama City, Hiroshima prefecture, he began writing poetry at middle school which found publication in the poetry column of the magazine *Wakakusa* (Young Grass; founded in 1925). The editor of the poetry column was Horiguchi Daigaku, whom the young poet took as his mentor and by whose *Gekka no Ichigun* he was strongly influenced. From the Waseda First High School he went to the Nagoya College of Pharmacy (1935–38) and afterwards returned to work in the family business for the rest of his life. While in Nagoya, he became a regular contributor to the local *Shibungaku Kenkyū* (Literary Studies), which was also the publisher of his first two collections, *Inaka no Shokutaku* (A Rustic Table, 1939) and *Umareta Ie* (The House Where I was Born,

1940). From 1944 he began to write *haiku* also, modelling himself on Kubota Mantarō (1889–1963). In 1949 he founded the poetry magazine *Kigutsu* (Clogs), which continued until his death. The definitive edition of his poems (1965) gained the eighteenth Yomiuri Prize for Literature in 1966. A modern sensibility shows through the traditional natural setting which forms the background to almost all of his poems.

Kitagawa Fuyuhiko is the pen-name of Taguro Tadahiko, born on 3 June 1900 in Ōtsu, Shiga prefecture. He grew up in Manchuria, where his father became an employee of the Manchurian Railway Company after the Russo-Japanese War. He returned to the Third Higher School in Kyoto and went on to study French Law at Tokyo Imperial University (1922–25). On graduation he entered the Department of French Literature to the annoyance of his father, who cut off his allowance. He was already coming into prominence in poetry circles; he had founded (1924) in Dairen, with Anzai Fuyue (1898–1965) and others, the magazine *A*, which continued until 1927 and which was the first of a number of magazines through which Kitagawa and his group led a revolution of the forms of modern poetry. He supported himself by translation and film criticism and began to publish the first of his many volumes of poetry. In 1928 he joined with Haruyama Yukio (b. 1902) in the founding of *Shi to Shiron* (Poetry and Poetics). After publishing the first series of *Jikan* (Time, 1930–31), with which his name is particularly associated, he was drawn into the Proletarian Literature movement of the early 1930s. After the war before reviving *Jikan* (May 1950–), he joined with Anzai Fuyue, Murano Shirō, and others in *Gendaishi* (Contemporary Poetry, February 1946–June 1950). In the post-war years he was a proponent of the long descriptive poem and neo-realism. He also published a modern translation of Dante's *Purgatorio* (1953).

Kitahara Hakushū (25 January 1885–2 November 1942). Born in Okinohata Village (now part of Yanagawa City) in Fukuoka prefecture, Kyūshū, into a *sake*-brewing family, Hakushū was early attracted to poetry and had contributed *tanka* to the *Fukuoka Nichinichi Shinbun* (Fukuoka Daily News) before enrolling in the Faculty of Literature at

Waseda University in 1904. In Tokyo he quickly attracted attention with a long poem in the magazine *Bunko* (Library) and by winning a poetry competition in the *Waseda Gakuhō* (Gazette). On Yosano Tekkan's invitation he joined the New Poetry Society and became a contributor to *Myōjō* in 1906. The expedition of *Myōjō* poets to Kyūshū in 1907 produced Hakushū's first collection, *Jashūmon* (The Heretical School, i.e., Christianity, March 1909), and established him as a leading figure of the poetry world. His second collection, *Omoide* (Reminiscences, 1911), of short lyric poems is more generally characteristic of his style. Though it is possible to set 1916 as the limit of his most historically significant activity, Hakushū's output in a wide variety of genres, *shi, tanka, haiku,* children's poems, folk songs, continued virtually all through his life and earned him the designation *kokumin shijin* (national poet). Of modern poets he was the most successful in exploiting the musical possibilities of the language, but it is a usual criticism to hold that he did this at the expense of intellectual content.

Kitamura Tarō was born on 17 November 1922 in Yanaka, Tokyo. He began to write poetry in 1937 while at the Third Tokyo Commercial School, from which he graduated in 1940. After the war he graduated in French literature from the University of Tokyo (1949) and joined the *Asahi* newspaper. Before the war he contributed to *Shin-ryōdo* (New Territory) and other magazines under his original name of Matsumura Fumio, and came to know Ayukawa Nobuo, Nakagiri Masao, and Tamura Ryūichi, with whom he was associated in the *Arechi* group in the early post-war period, Kitamura's *oeuvre* is very small; the latest version of his *Poetical Works* (1975) still contains less than fifty poems, but his work enjoys a high reputation for the perfection of its diction and metrical skill.

Kōra Rumiko was born on 16 December 1932 in Tokyo, where she graduated from Keiō University. Recognition for her poetry came with her collection *Basho* (The Place, 1962), which gained her the thirteenth Mr H. Prize in 1963. She is now regarded as one of the leading women poets (she appeared in the Shichōsha *Modern Poetry Library* in 1971).

Kuroda Kio was born on 28 February 1926 in Yonezawa, Yamagata prefecture, and grew up in Sagae in the same prefecture. He attended school only as far as higher primary. During the war he worked as a labourer in the Tokyo–Yokohama area, and at this time learned Russian and read Russian and proletarian literature. He went home after the war and fell ill while an activist in the farmers movement. In the early 1950s he became involved in the movement of the *Rettō* (Archipelago) group of Sekine Hiroshi (b. 1920), Hasegawa Ryūsei, and others and began to write poems. He joined the editorial staff of the magazines *Gendaishi* (Contemporary Poetry) and *Eiga Hihyō* (Film Criticism). He published his first collection, *Fuan to Yūgeki* (Alarms and Excursions), in 1959, followed by *Chichū no Buki* (Arms in the Earth, 1961) and a *Poetical Works* in 1966. *Fuan to Yūgeki* won him the tenth Mr H. Prize in 1960. His gift of fantasy is unique among poets of the Left.

Kuroda Saburō was born on 26 February 1919 in the naval-base town of Kure in Hiroshima prefecture. From the Seventh Higher School (Kagoshima) he went on to Tokyo Imperial University, where he graduated from the Faculty of Economics. During the war he was posted to Java as an employee of the South Seas Development Corporation. Since the war he has worked for the Japan Broadcasting Corporation (NHK). While at the Seventh Higher School he began to contribute to Kitasono Katsue's *VOU*. After the war he became a member of the *Arechi* (Waste Land) group, and when it broke up, like others joined Kusano Shinpei's *Rekitei*. His first published collection, *Hitori no Onna ni* (À une femme, 1954), an outstanding volume of love poems, gained him the fifth Mr H. Prize in 1955. In the same year he published thirty surviving pre-1942 poems as a collection entitled *Ushinawareta Bohimei* (Lost Epitaphs). Several other volumes have followed, as well as two books of criticism.

Kusano Shinpei was born on 12 May 1903, the second of three sons, all of whom were to gain some reputation as poets, of a small landowning family in Kami-ogawa village, Fukushima prefecture. Brought up by his grandparents while the family lived in Tokyo, he failed to complete middle school. He gained admission to a general studies course at

Keiō University in 1920 but withdrew after six months. In the next year, through the help of a friend of his father, he went to Canton, where he worked and at the same time studied at Ling-nan University. His stay in Canton (until July 1925 with a number of visits home to Japan in the interim) was decisive in turning him to poetry. He learned English and discovered new American poetry, especially that of Carl Sandburg. In Hong Kong he met Rabīndranāth Tagore on his way to lecture in China (1924); in Japan he visited Yamamura Bochō not long before his death. In April 1925 he launched from Canton the important coterie magazine *Dora* (Gong), and in the same year his thirty-year friendship with Takamura Kōtarō began. During the next ten years, though his personal circumstances were not easy, he established himself as a leading figure in the world of poetry and was one of the founders of *Rekitei* (The Course of History) in 1935. He continued to publish poetry during his war years (1940–45) as an adviser to the Wang Ching-wei government in Nanking. In the post-war years he has lengthened the long list of his volumes of poems and has edited the collected works of Takamura Kōtarō, Yagi Jūkichi (1898–1927), and Miyazawa Kenji and volumes of studies upon them. His poetic expression moved from an early anarchism to his characteristic fauvism with its favourite frog image. His fantasies are supported by a sense of universality.

Maruyama Kaoru (8 June 1899–21 October 1974). Maruyama was born in Ōita, Kyūshū, where his father was then stationed. The many moves in his early years, occasioned by his father's changes of post (Nagasaki, Tokyo, Seoul, Tokyo, Matsue, and Tokyo again by the time he was twelve), he claims, gave him a feeling of being a perpetual stranger. After his father's death he lived in his grandfather's home in Toyohashi in Aichi prefecture, and here he had his middle school education. A passion for the works of Charles Kingsley, Stevenson, and Conrad aroused in him a desire to become a sailor, and he entered the Tokyo Merchant Marine High School in 1917. Illness forced him to withdraw in the next year, and in 1921 he entered the Third Higher School (Kyoto) where he became friends with Miyoshi Tatsuji. In 1925 he went on to the Department of Japanese Literature in Tokyo Imperial University. He left without graduating three years later, but he had begun to devote himself to poetry. He published his first collection *Ho, Ranpu, Kamome* (Sails, Lamps and Gulls) in 1932. This has been regarded as marking a new departure in modern Japanese poetry "with its unique lyric spirit and style", and in 1934 he joined with Miyoshi Tatsuji and Hori Tatsuo (1904–53) in founding *Shiki* (Four Seasons) which represented the main stream of poetry through the rest of the 1930s. During the war he had his long-desired sea experience as a special correspondent in a training ship. In the post-war period he became a lecturer (later professor) at Aichi University. He continued to publish collections of poems through the 1950s and 1960s with frequent recurrence to his sea theme and an increasing realism and directness of expression.

Matsushima Mami: no biographical details available. She appears to have been a student in Kyoto at the time of her contribution to *Nobi* (Wildfire, 1965).

Miki Rofū (23 June 1889–21 December 1964). Born in what is now Tatsuno City, Hyōgo prefecture, he contributed poems to established magazines while still a schoolboy, and his first collection was published at his own expense when he was sixteen. In 1907, on the eve of entering the Faculty of Literature at Waseda University (he later, in 1910, also studied at Keiō), he joined in the formation of the Waseda Poetry Society and became a contributor to *Waseda Bungaku*, in which in the following year he published one of the first poems to be written in colloquial as opposed to literary Japanese. This, like other colloquial poems of the time, was merely experimental, and his general style remained literary. In his second and third collections, *Haien* (Deserted Garden, 1909) and *Sabishiki Akebono* (Lonely Dawn, 1910), he turned to symbolism and became known with Kitahara Hakushū as leader of the movement. The two poets published a joint collection, *Wasurenagusa* (Forget-me-not), as a special number of the magazine *Zanboa* (Pomelo) in 1912. The next decade brought further volumes of poetry, the founding of the Miraisha (Futurist Society) and three attempts to publish its magazine *Mirai*, and an increasing interest by Rofū in religion. He was received into the Catholic Church in 1922. His later volumes between 1915 and 1926 are of religious verse.

Mitsui (Saijō) Futabako was born in 1919 in Tokyo, daughter of Saijō Yaso (1892–1970), already a modern poet (he published his first collection in the year of Futabako's birth) and later Professor of French Literature at Waseda University and known as a writer of popular songs. She graduated in English Literature from the Japan Women's College. While a student, she contributed poems to *Rō-ningyō* (Wax Dolls; ran 1930–44), edited by her father. After the war she collaborated with him in publishing *Poet Lore*, which ran for nine issues from 1952. She published her collection *Kō-hankyū* (Rear Hemisphere) in 1957.

Miyazawa Kenji (27 August 1896–21 September 1933). Born into a wealthy, talented and devoutly Buddhist family in Hanamaki, Iwate prefecture, in northern Japan, after middle school in Morioka, the prefectural capital, he entered the Higher Agriculture and Forestry School there. On graduation in 1918 he continued as a postgraduate student and made an important soil survey of his local area. Then he became attracted to a new Nichiren-based sect of Buddhism and in 1921 went to Tokyo to join in its activities. The illness of his sister Toshi (1898–1922) brought him home, and he became a teacher in the local agricultural school (until 1926). He began to write poetry and in 1924 published at his own expense the first series of *Haru to Shura* (Spring and Asura), the only collection of his poems to appear in his lifetime. In the same year he published *Chūmon no Ōi Ryōriten* (The Restaurant with Many Orders), a collection of the children's stories for which he was to become equally known. *Haru to Shura* caught the attention of Kusano Shinpei, who invited him to join his *Dora* group. It was Kusano who with Takamura Kōtarō and others brought the bulk of Miyazawa's work to publication after his death. For most of the rest of his life he lived as a farmer, founding a local society to work for the improvement of the agriculture of the district. He was a rare combination of thinker and man of action, a skilled linguist and scientist who could embrace Beethoven and Buddhism, a compulsive worker who yet revealed a great capacity for humour.

Miyoshi Tatsuji (23 August 1900–5 April 1964). The son of an Ōsaka printer, he first started on a career as a professional soldier and entered the Ōsaka Area Military Preparatory School at the age of fifteen. He had progressed as far as the Military Academy when in 1921 he withdrew and returned home to Ōsaka. He had already studied French and written many *haiku*. He quarrelled with his father and went to live with the family of an aunt in Kōbe. The family supported his studies at the Third Higher School in Kyoto (1922–25) and afterwards in the Department of French at Tokyo Imperial University, from which he graduated in 1928. On the activities and associations of these years Miyoshi's literary career was firmly founded. He supported himself first as a translator: he undertook Zola's *Nana* for a series on world literature in 1929, Baudelaire's *Spleen de Paris* (completed in 1928, but also published in 1929), and Jean-Henri Fabre's *Souvenirs entomologiques* in 1930. Later he was to translate Baudelaire's *Fleurs du mal* (1935) and Francis Jammes's *Les Nuits qui me chantent* (1936). The first of his twenty volumes of poems, *Sokuryō-sen* (Survey Ship), appeared in 1930, the last in 1952. In 1934 with Hori Tatsuo (1904–53) and Maruyama Kaoru he founded the monthly poetry magazine *Shiki* (Four Seasons) which continued until June 1944. Miyoshi's poetry is notable for its combination of traditional lyric qualities and a modern Western sensibility such that one may hear echoes of the great Chinese poets subtly blending with those of modern France. He collaborated with the eminent sinologist Yoshikawa Kōjirō in *Shin Tōshi Sen* (New Anthology of T'ang Poems, 1952). The definitive edition of his complete poetical works was published in 1962 and awarded the Yomiuri Prize for Literature in the following January.

Miyoshi Toyoichirō was born on 25 August 1920 in Hachiōji on the western outskirts of Tokyo. He graduated from the Faculty of Political Science and Economics at Waseda University. As a youth he had wanted to become a painter but turned to poetry under the influence of Kitahara Hakushū's work. He began to publish before the war in *Shin-ryōdo* (New Territory) and was drawn into the circle of Ayukawa Nobuo, which formed the nucleus of the post-war *Arechi* group. Illness kept him from military service, but his wartime poems, collected in *Shūjin* (The Prisoner, 1949) greatly impressed the critics and have been described as "the earliest authentic post-war poems".

Mori Michiyo was born on 15 April 1901 in Mie prefecture. She was a student at the Tokyo Women's Higher Normal School when she met Kaneko Mitsuharu and soon after married him in 1924. She published her first volume of poems, *Ryūnyo no Hitomi* (The Pupils of the Eyes of the Dragon King's Daughter), in March 1927 and a second volume in collaboration with her husband two months later (*Fuka Shizumu*, The Shark Sinks). A third volume, *Tōhō no Shi* (Poems of the East, 1934), resulted from her travels through Asia to Europe with Kaneko. In the early 1940s she turned to fiction and achieved a reputation in this field also. In later years her effort has been directed to the retelling of Japanese and Western classics for children.

Murano Shirō (7 October 1901–2 March 1975). Born in the village of Tama on the outskirts of Tokyo, Murano inherited his father's enthusiasm for *haiku*. He came to *shi* through a knowledge of modern German poetry and the influence of Hagiwara Sakutarō's early collections, while studying economics at Keiō University (1921–27). By the time he graduated he had published his first collection, *Wana* (Snare, 1926). After a year as a volunteer, during which he served with the First Regiment of Foot Guards, from 1929 he worked for the Physical and Chemical Research Combine up to and during the war. From the 1930s he was prominent in the organization of poetry groups and magazines. On the founding of the Modern Poetry Society in 1949 he became assistant secretary-general, and in 1960 he was elected president of the Modern Poetry Society of Japan. Besides his nine volumes of poems, brought together in a *Complete Poems* in 1968, he published several books of criticism, for he believed that poetry and criticism should go hand in hand. He described his own poetic progress as an attempt to attain a special aesthetic world, starting out from modern lyricism.

Murō Saisei (1 August 1889–26 March 1962). Saisei was born in Kanazawa, the son of a former samurai and a maid. Handed over to foster-parents, he spent a childhood marred by hatred of his foster-mother and his teacher; he left school in the third year of higher primary (1904). He began work as an usher in the local law-court. As he slowly improved his position, he developed a passion for reading and was instructed in writing *haiku* by one of his superiors. After he had begun to publish *haiku* and essays, he went to Tokyo (1910) and for several years lived a life of extreme poverty, alternating between the capital and Kanazawa, but becoming increasingly known in poetry circles. In 1914 he joined with Hagiwara Sakutarō and Yamamura Bochō in the Ningyo-shisha (Mermaid Society) and in 1916 with Hagiwara in a Kanjo-shisha, publishing the magazine *Kanjō* (Feelings). He published his first collection, *Ai no Shishū* (Love Poems), under this society's imprimatur in 1918 with the aid of a small legacy from his foster-father, who had died the year before. The small printing sold quickly, and he was able to print in the same year his second collection *Jojō-shōkyoku-shū* (Anthology of Short Lyrics), which had great influence on the poets of the next generation. He followed his success in poetry with an immediate success in autobiographical fiction with *Yōnen Jidai* (Childhood) and *Sei ni Mezameru Koro* (Awakening to Sex), both first published in *Chūōkōron* (Central Review) in 1919. Through the next four decades he continued with varying success to produce poetry and fiction, as well as essays and critical works, including *Waga Aisuru Shijin no Denki* (Biographies of the Poets I Love, 1958).

Mushanokōji Saneatsu (12 May 1885–9 April 1976). Born into an aristocratic family in the Kōjimachi ward of Tokyo, he was educated at the Peers' School, where he first met Shiga Naoya (1883–1971) and Arishima Takeo (1878–1923) and others with whom he was later to be associated in the *Shirakaba* group. He began to study sociology at Tokyo Imperial University in 1905 but gave up in the following year. In 1910 Mushanokōji joined with his young friends in *Shirakaba* (White Birch) which until its demise in 1923 held a major place in the cultural life of the Taishō era: it embraced literature and art, drama and music. He not only expressed his humanist and individualist beliefs in his writings but also attempted to translate them into action in the founding of his "New Village" in Kyūshū in 1918 as a model for a new society. Though poetry was a more minor part of his writing than novels, plays, and critical essays, he published collections of poems in 1920, 1930, and 1946.

Nagase Kiyoko was born on 17 February 1906 in Toyoda village in Okayama prefecture. In 1922 the family moved to Nagoya, where she graduated in English from the Aichi Prefectural First Girls' High School (1927). She had begun to write poetry when she was eighteen and to publish in *Shi no Ie* (House of Poetry), edited by Satō Sōnosuke (1890–1942) and the Nagoya coterie magazine *Shinsei* (New Life). In 1927 she married and went to live in Ōsaka. Her first poetry collection, *Gurenderu no Hahaoya* (Grendel's Mother), was published in 1930. In the next year she went to Tokyo and became a contributor to Kitagawa Fuyuhiko's first *Jikan* (Time, April 1930–June 1931) and afterwards to his *Jiba* (Magnetic Field, September 1931–April 1932) and *Pan* (Bread, October 1933–January 1938). In 1945 she fled from devastated Tokyo back to her native Okayama and for the next twenty years and more engaged in agriculture, while continuing to produce many volumes of poems. She has described the difficulties for a woman poet in pre-war Japan in her collection of essays *Onna-shijin no Techō* (A Woman Poet's Notebook, 1952).

Nagashima Miyoshi was born on 14 September 1917 in Uraga, Yokosuka, at the entrance to Tokyo Bay, and graduated from Yokohama College. He was conscripted into the army in 1937 and fought in China, where he was wounded and repatriated to Japan. His battle experiences had a lasting effect on his poetry. His *Kuroi Kajitsu* (Black Fruit, 1951) gained him the Mr H. Prize for 1952.

Nakae Toshio was born on 1 February 1933 in Kurume, Fukuoka prefecture. He graduated in Japanese Literature from Kansai University in Ōsaka. When he began to write poetry, he knew nothing of existing magazines and coteries but worked under the guidance by correspondence of Nagase Kiyoko, Amano Tadashi (b. 1909), and Takamura Satoru. He published his first volume of poems *Uo no naka no Jikan* (Time Among the Fishes) in 1952 at the age of nineteen. In 1954, as a result of winning an *Arechi* Poets Prize, he began to publish in the *Arechi* anthologies, and in the same year on the invitation of Tanikawa Shuntarō and Kawasaki Hiroshi (b. 1930) he joined *Kai* (Oar). During the second half of the 1950s and the 1960s he produced a further five volumes of poems.

Nakagiri Masao was born on 11 October 1919 at a colliery in Fukuoka prefecture (sometimes wrongly said to have been born in Kurashiki, Okayama prefecture, because of his familty registration) but grew up in Kōbe. He graduated in Fine Arts from Nihon University, Tokyo. From 1942 to 1968 he worked, mainly as a political reporter, for the *Yomiuri* newspaper. He is now a lecturer at Hōsei University. In 1937 he founded the magazine *Luna* (afterwards renamed *Le Bal* and later *Shishū*, Anthology), which was an important forerunner of *Arechi* (Waste Land) in its post-war form. Nakagiri joined the *Arechi* group and also contributed to *Rekitei*. His *Poetical Works* (1964) received the Takamura Kōtarō Prize for the following year. He has been active in the introduction of contemporary English and American poetry. He has published *Kiki no Shijin* (Poets of Crisis, an anthology of English poets of the 1930s, 1953), *Anthology of Contemporary English Poetry* (1963), and translations of W. H. Auden's poems and critical essays.

Nakahara Chūya (29 April 1907–22 October 1937). The son of an army doctor who had attempted fiction under the influence of Mori Ōgai, Nakahara was born in Yamaguchi, where his father had married the daughter of an important local family. His early life was marked by frequent moves on account of his father's postings. In spite of an early reputation as a genius and although he published *tanka* at sixteen, his record in middle school in Yamaguchi declined until he failed his third year (1923). He was sent away to the private Ritsumeikan Middle School in Kyoto, and from this time his poetic career fully began. He first fell under the influence of Takahashi Shinkichi's Dadaism; then Tominaga Tarō (1901–25) introduced him to French symbolism. He also began to live with a young film-actress, Hasegawa Yasuko, who later left him for his friend, the critic Kobayashi Hideo (b. 1902). Yasuko has an important part in Nakahara's poetry. They went to Tokyo together in 1925, where he advanced in the literary world, while seeking university entrance (he finally graduated from the School of Foreign Languages in 1933). In 1929 he founded the coterie magazine *Hakuchi-gun* (Idiot Group). which ran for six numbers. In 1934 he became a member of the *Shiki* (Four Seasons) group and in the next year joined Kusano Shinpei's *Rekitei*. His first collection, *Yagi no*

Uta (Goat's Songs), was published in 1934; his second, *Arishi-hi no Uta* (Songs of the Days That Were), posthumously in 1938.

Nakamura Minoru was born on 17 January 1927 in Ōmiya, Saitama prefecture. He graduated from the Faculty of Law of the University of Tokyo and since 1952 has practised as a lawyer. He began to write poetry while at the First Higher School in Tokyo with the encouragement of fellow students such as Iida Momo, with whom he was to join in his university days in founding the magazine *Sedai* (Generation), which ran for six years (1946–52). In the same period he also contributed to *Shigaku* (Poetry Studies) and *Hihyō* (Criticism). His collection *Mugon-ka* (Songs without Words, 1950) was among the first to be published by a post-war poet. He followed this with *Ki* (Tree, 1954) and *Ubara-shō* (Ubara Anthology, 1966). His poems are admired for the elegant correctness of their language. He has also published studies of Miyazawa Kenji and Nakahara Chūya, the two poets who were his early influences.

Nakano Shigeharu was born on 25 January 1902 into a farming family in Takaboko village in Fukui prefecture on the western coast of the main island of Japan. He was brought up by his grandparents because his father, who worked for the Tobacco Monopoly Bureau, was often away from home. After middle school in Fukui he went on in 1912 to the Fourth Higher School in Kanazawa, where his interest in poetry developed. He was especially attracted to Murō Saisei and the *tanka* poet Saitō Mokichi (1882–1953), on whom he was to publish a critical study in 1942. He graduated after two extra years in 1924 and entered the Department of German Literature at Tokyo Imperial University. Here he founded the coterie magazine *Razō* (Nude, 1925), in which he published twenty of the poems that make up his small *oeuvre*. Friendship with Hayashi Fusao (b. 1903) brought him into the New Man Society (Shinjinkai) and introduced him to Marxism. *Razō* was followed by *Roba* (Donkey, 1926) which achieved twelve numbers, and after Nakano's graduation in 1927 by *Puroretaria Geijutsu* (Proletarian Art). He remained a leading figure in the various organizations of the Proletarian Literature movement until the time of his second arrest in 1933. The first edition of his collected poems in 1931 was confiscated, and from a second edition in 1935 about a third was expurgated: the first complete edition appeared in 1947. His later effort has lain in fiction and criticism, but his poems, which combine a lyric feeling with a spirit of social criticism, are by common consent the outstanding examples of "proletarian poetry".

Nishio Katsuko was born in 1923 in Hokkaidō but grew up in Karafuto (Sakhalin), where she graduated from the Toyohara Girls' High School. She began writing poetry in middle age and in 1971 became a member of the *Jikan* (Time) group.

Nishiwaki Junzaburō was born on 20 January 1894 in Ojiya, Niigata prefecture, where his father was the local banker. An enthusiast for English in his middle school days, he left for Tokyo after graduation (1911) with the idea of becoming a painter. He was well received by Kuroda Seiki (1866–1924) and welcomed into his White Horse school of Western painting. The life of an art student, however, seems to have been uncongenial, and his father's death may also have influenced his decision to study economics at Keiō University, from which he graduated in 1917. Throughout he had maintained his interest in Western literature, art, and philosophy. After working for the *Japan Times* and then the Foreign Office, he became a teacher in the preparatory course at Keiō (1920). In 1922 he left for England, arriving too late to be admitted that year to Oxford, where he studied Early and Mediaeval English (1923–25), but the year of waiting in London at a time when Eliot's *Waste Land* and Joyce's *Ulysses* were newly published was not wasted. In 1925 his first book of poems in English, *Spectrum*, was published in London, before he returned to Keiō to become a professor of English Literature (1926). Another volume of poems in English (*Poems Barbarous*, 1930) preceded his first Japanese collection, *Ambarvalia* (1933), but he had already become the centre of a new surrealist movement and an important theorist in the magazine *Shi to Shiron* (Poetry and Poetics, 1928–31). After *Ambarvalia*, his next volume did not appear until after the war. In 1947 he published *Tabibito Kaerazu* (The Traveller Does Not Return) and entered on a very active period of publication: a three-volume *History of Modern English Literature* (1948), translations of Chaucer's *Canterbury Tales* (1949) and Eliot's *Waste Land* (1952), a further six volumes of poetry, culminating in a *Complete Poetical Works* in 1963 (an additional collection, *Reiki*, The Record of the Rites, appeared in 1967), and his *Poetics* (*Shigaku*, 1969).

Noma Fumiyo was born c. 1945 in Nagasaki. She escaped death from the atomic bomb which destroyed her home and killed her relatives because her mother had gone out shopping with the child on her back. Her poem *Makoto no Imi* (The Real Meaning) has thus a personal basis.

Ono Tōzaburō was born on 27 July 1903 in Ōsaka, where he attended middle school, although his early childhood was spent in Nara. In 1920 he went to Tokyo and entered Tōyō University. He gave up after eight months, but in this time he had found his way into anarchist-socialist circles. In 1923 he became a contributor to the newly founded *Aka to Kuro* (Red and Black). When this ceased in 1924, he founded his own Dadaist-anarchist *Dam Dam* but produced only one issue. After publishing his first volume of poems, *Hanbun Hiraita Mado* (The Half-opened Window), at his own expense in 1926, he again attempted an anarchist magazine, *Dandō* (Trajectory), which survived for a year (1930–31), in association with Akiyama Kiyoshi (b. 1904). In 1933 he returned to Ōsaka; the industrial landscape of Ōsaka is the background of many of his later poems. Here in the post-war period he was to become the acknowledged leader and teacher of younger poets. He gradually shifted to a Marxist-realist position in his *Furuki Sekai no ue ni* (Above the Old World, 1934) and *Ōsaka* (1939) and also turned to criticism, with which he was to exert a major influence. He published successive essays in the magazine *Bunka Soshiki* (Organization of Culture, 1940–43), which were brought together in *Shiron* (Essays on Poetry, 1947; definitive edition 1949). He sought to reject musical quality and to replace *tanka*-type lyricism by a lyricism founded on a critical and rational spirit. His post-war collections include *Daikai-hen* (The Ocean's Edge, 1947), *Hi-nomu Keyaki* (Fire-swallowing Zelkova,

1952), *Jūyu Fuji* (Fuji of Heavy Oil, 1956), and *Ikyō* (Strange Land, 1966).

Ōoka Makoto was born on 16 February 1931 in Mishima, Shizuoka prefecture, south-west of Tokyo. He graduated in Japanese Literature from the University of Tokyo. He worked for ten years (1953–63) in the foreign news department of the *Yomiuri* newspaper and afterwards became an assistant professor at Meiji University. During the 1950s he was a member of the *Kai* (Oar), *Konnichi* (Today), and *Wani* (Crocodile) groups. His published volumes of poems begin with *Kioku to Genzai* (Memory and the Present, 1956). He is also the author of a large number of studies of poetry as well as of works on modern Western artists.

Ozaki Kihachi (31 January 1892–4 February 1974). Born in Tokyo, he was put out to nurse, because his businessman father divorced his mother. Though he was taken back at the age of four, he was treated as an adopted son. He graduated from a commercial school, which gave him a knowledge of English, and at seventeen began to work in a bank. He became an avid reader of European literature in English translation, in particular of Tolstoy, and also of the works of the *Shirakaba* group, which were then beginning to appear. He came to know Takamura Kōtarō and was inspired by his translation of *Jean Christophe*. Ozaki's first publication was of Romain Rolland's music criticism in *Shirakaba* in 1916. Under the influence of Takamura and Senke Motomaro he began to write poetry (1920) and to them he dedicated his first volume of poems, *Sora to Jumoku* (Sky and Trees, 1922). His efforts to aid his father in the great Kantō earthquake of 1923 brought a reconciliation between them (he had earlier been disinherited for his pursuit of literature and a love-affair of which his father disapproved). His circumstances now became easier. Living usually in rural surroundings on the outskirts of Tokyo, he produced some ten volumes of poetry and prose-essays as well as translations from French and German, especially of Georges Duhamel and Hermann Hesse. A nature poet who expressed himself in very ordinary language, he had a more metaphysical quality than his mentors Takamura and Senke.

Saga Nobuyuki was born on 18 April 1902 in Miyakonojō, Miyazaki prefecture, in southeast Kyūshū. He has worked in magazine publishing since he began with *Bungei Shunjū* in its early period under Kikuchi Kan (1923–39); finally he joined *Shigaku* (Poetry Studies). He began contributing poetry to Kusano Shinpei's *Rekitei* in the post-war period and has published two volumes of metaphysical poems, *Ai to Shi no Kazoe-uta* (Counting-out Rhymes on Love and Death, 1957) and *Tamashii no naka no Shi* (Death in the Soul, 1966).

Satō Haruo (9 April 1892–6 May 1964) was born in Shingū, Wakayama prefecture. Both his father and grandfather were doctors but also known for their fondness for poetry (*haiku* and Chinese poems). Haruo early declared himself for literature. While still in middle school he had *tanka* published in *Myōjō* and *Subaru* (The Pleiades), and when he went to Tokyo after graduating (1910) he was accepted into the New Poetry Society. In the same year he entered Keiō University, and though he gave up five years later (1914) without a degree he had been a frequent contributor to *Subaru* and *Mita Bungaku* of poems and critical essays. His early work contains poems on social questions as well as the lyrics which became characteristic of him. Financial difficulties forced a temporary retreat to the country in 1916, but this produced the autobiographical novel *Den'en no Yūutsu* (The Melancholy of the Country, definitive ed. 1919), which secured his reputation as a writer of fiction (in which his output was large). He became an established Shinchōsha author, and the same publisher brought out his first and second collections of poetry, *Junjō-shishū* (Sentimental Poems, 1921) and *Waga Sen Kyūhyaku Nijū-ni Nen* (My 1922, 1923). In 1926 he added a third strand to his eminence in Taishō letters with the publication of his volume of criticism *Taikutsu Tokuhon* (Readings in Ennui).

Senke Motomaro (8 June 1888–14 March 1948) was born in aristocratic surroundings in Kōjimachi, Tokyo. His father was Baron Senke Takatomi, who rose through prefectural governorships and the governorship of Tokyo to be minister of justice in the Saionji cabinet of 1906; his mother enjoyed some reputation as a painter. He achieved poor school results and did not complete middle school, but by the age of sixteen he was writing *shi*, *tanka*, and *haiku*. He found his way into literary society and in 1912 joined in publishing a coterie magazine *Terracotta*, through which he met Mushanokōji Saneatsu and was drawn into the *Shirakaba* group. Senke may be called the representative in poetry of the humanistic *Shirakaba* group, and the Taishō period (1912–26) was the high point of his career, though he continued to publish volumes of poems until 1939. His typical poems, written in a simple direct style, express a love of Nature and treat life in terms of affection and trust. They thus seem naive to the post-war generation.

Shibuya Haruo was born in 1924 in Karafuto (Sakhalin) and graduated in Economics from Tōhoku University in Sendai in 1949. He began writing poetry at the age of seventeen under the influence of Kitasono Katsue (b. 1902) and Nishiwaki Junzaburō. During the 1950s he was active in poetry circles in Sendai and edited several magazines there. He also published his first volume of poems, *The Fountain*, there in 1962. Afterwards he moved to Tokyo and became a member of the *Kaju-en* (Orchard) group.

Shimazaki Tōson (25 March 1872–22 August, 1943). Born in the village of Magome in Nagano prefecture, he was sent to Tokyo at the age of nine because his father thought that it would benefit his studies. After attending the Mita English School in Shiba and other schools, he graduated from the Christian-founded Meiji Gakuin in 1891 and in the next year became a teacher of English at the sister institution, the Meiji Women's College (Meiji Jogakkō). He had already published anonymously in *Jogaku Zasshi* (The Ladies Magazine) and in 1893 joined with his friend and fellow-teacher Kitamura Tōkoku (1868–1894) in the founding of *Bungakkai* (Literary World), an important organ for romanticism in this period. In 1896 a new academic appointment in Sendai removed him temporarily from the Tokyo scene, but he returned in the next year and in August his first poetry collection, *Wakana-shū* (Young Herbs), was published. *Wakana-shū* is generally regarded as the work that marks the success of the New Poetry movement and has gained Tōson an enduring reputation as a poet. Yet after three further volumes (1898–1901; the four collections were brought together in a *Poetical Works* in 1904), he left poetry for the novel, in which he gained his first success with *Hakai* (The Broken Commandment) in 1906.

Shinkawa Kazue was born on 22 April 1929 in Yūki, Ibaraki prefecture, where she graduated in 1946 from the local girls' high school. She began to write poetry in her school days with Saijō Yaso (1892 –1970) as her model. After moving to Tokyo in 1948, she published stories and children's poems in magazines for girls. Of her volumes of poems, *Rōma no Aki, Sonota* (Roman Autumn and Other Pieces) gained a Murō Saisei Prize in 1965, and the leading poet publishers Shichōsha issued a *Poetical Works* in 1975.

Shiraishi Kazuko was born on 27 February 1931 in Vancouver, Canada. She graduated in the History of Art from the Faculty of Letters of Waseda University. In her teens she joined the *VOU* group led by Kitasono Katsue (b. 1902), by whom she was introduced to modernism and surrealism. Later she stood apart from magazines and groups. Her first volume, *Tamago no Furu Machi* (Town under a Rainfall of Eggs), appeared in 1951 and has been followed by some five other volumes, including a *Poetical Works* in 1968.

Suyama Hisayo was born on 23 May 1882 in Hiroshima. Her poetical career began late in life in the post-war period, when she joined a local *haiku* society in Shōbara, Hiroshima prefecture. She published her first volume of poems *Asu to-iu Hi o* (Tomorrow!) in 1966 and a second collection, *Shii no Mi* (Acorn), in the next year.

Tada Chimako was born in 1930 and graduated from Keiō University. She published her first volume of poems, *Hanabi* (Fireworks), in 1956. Besides her poetry, she is well known for her translations, in particular of the poems of Saint-John Perse.

Takagi Kyōzō was born in 1903 in Aomori, at the extreme northern end of the main island of Japan. After working for a local newspaper and then (1927) for a small publisher in Tokyo, he went to Manchuria and entered the Medical College at Fengtien. On graduation he pursued a medical career in Manchuria and after the war in Japan. He began writing poems in his native Tsugaru dialect in 1926 and took as his model the poems appearing in the magazine *A*, which Kitagawa Fuyuhiko and Anzai Fuyue had founded in Dairen in 1924. He came to know Anzai Fuyue after he moved to Manchuria. His first volume of poems, *Marmelo* (Quince), was published in 1931 but went unnoticed until a second edition in 1953 brought a wide response for its successful use of dialect. In his two later pre-war volumes and in his post-war *Poems That Are Not Poems by a Poet Who Is Not a Poet* (1965), which he says were stimulated by Nishiwaki Junzaburō's translation of *The Waste Land*, he turned to writing in standard Japanese.

Takahashi Mutsuo was born on 15 December 1937 in what is now the city of Kitakyūshū. After a long recovery from tuberculosis in his early twenties he went to Tokyo and worked for the Tokyo Design Centre. Besides the collections *Bara no Ki: Nise no Koibitotachi* (Rose Tree: Imitation Lovers, 1964), *Nemuri to Okashi to Rakka to* (Slumber, and Sin and Fall, 1965), and *Yogoretaru-mono wa sarani Yogoretaru koto o Nase* (You Dirty Ones, Do Even Dirtier Things!, 1966), he has published an autobiographical novel.

Takahashi Shinkichi was born on 28 January 1901 in Ikata, a fishing village in Ehime prefecture, Shikoku, where his father was headmaster of the primary school. His formal education ended at the age of seventeen (1918) when he withdrew from the Yawatahama Commercial School just before graduation after a visit to Tokyo without his father's permission. On a second visit in 1919 he caught typhus and spent two months in hospital. His introduction to Dadaism, of which he was a Japanese pioneer, came through a local Yawatahama newspaper in 1920. The year 1921 was significant in his life, for he spent February to September in a Shingon (esoteric Buddhist) temple and then went again to Tokyo. Here he produced a mimeographed collection of poems, *Makuwa-uri Shishū* (Melon Anthology), and became acquainted with Satō Haruo and with Hirado Renkichi (1893–1922), who issued his Futurist Manifesto in this year. His own Dadaist Manifesto appeared in *Shūkan Nihon* (Weekly Japan) in July 1922, and in September he published three Dada poems in the magazine *Kaizō* (Reconstruction). His collection *The Poems of Dadaist Shinkichi*, which established his reputation, came out in 1923. In 1928 he began his training in Zen, which has shaped his later life and poetry. Besides his many volumes of poetry and works on Zen, he has published fiction, essays, an autobiography, and lately studies on art.

Takami Jun (18 February, 1907–17 August 1965). Born in Fukui prefecture, of which his natural father (uncle of the novelist and translator of French poetry Nagai Kafū 1879–1959) was governor, Takami grew up in Tokyo, where he graduated from the First Higher School and the Department of English Literature of the Imperial University (1930). He was drawn into the Proletarian Literature movement and arrested under the Peace Preservation Law in 1933. It was with an outstanding "conversion" novel, *Kokyū Wasureubeki* (Should Auld Acquaintance be Forgot?, 1935), that he established himself as a writer of fiction. During the war years he was conscripted and assigned to the news service, first in South-east Asia and later in Hankow and Shanghai. His main effort in poetry dates from the post-war period, when he published *Jumoku-ha* (Tree Group, 1950), *Waga Maisō* (My Burial, 1963), and *Shi no Fuchi yori* (From the Abyss of Death, 1964), for he regarded poetry as the literature for old age, not only for youth. At the same time he continued to write prize-winning novels and works of criticism.

Takamura Kōtarō (originally Mitsutarō) (13 March 1883–2 April 1956). Born in the Shitaya ward of Tokyo, eldest son of Takamura Kōun (1852–1934), a great master of traditional Japanese wood-sculpture, he was both a pioneer in the introduction and adaptation of Western sculpture in Japan and a major modern poet. Kōtarō's twofold interest in art and poetry was established in his years at the Tokyo Art School (1897–1905), where he first developed his enthusiasm for the work of Auguste Rodin and at the same time became a member of the New Poetry Society and contributed *tanka* to *Myōjō*. He returned from study in New York, London, Paris, and Italy (1906–9) to practise sculpture and oil-painting and in time to join in the activity of the Pan Society. The year 1914 saw the publication of his first collection of poems, *Dōtei* (Journey) and his marriage to Naganuma Chieko. His collection *Chieko-shō* (1941) records their love through his wife's tragic breakdown, attempted suicide, and final death in 1938. *Tenkei* (Specimen), the most important of his later volumes of poems, appeared in 1950. His varied literary output includes translations of Verhaeren (*Akarui Toki, Les Heures claires*, 1921; *Tenjō no Honoo, Les Flammes hautes*, 1925) and of Rodin (*Rodin no Kotoba*, 1916) and volumes of essays on art such as *Bi ni tsuite* (On Art, 1941) and *Zōkeibi-ron* (On the Plastic Arts, 1942). Takamura seems to have been able to sustain the quality and freshness of his poetry throughout his life because of the strength of his style and the independence of his position.

Takano Kikuo was born on 20 November 1927 on Sado Island. He graduated from the Utsunomiya (Tokyo) College of Agriculture and Forestry and is a school teacher by profession. He began writing poetry in 1946 but is said to have burned the output of his first five years. In 1953 he joined the *Arechi* (Waste Land) group and began writing again. A feeling of spiritual isolation and a continual quest for understanding of existence set him at the extremity of the *Arechi* movement. He has published three collections: *Koma* (Top, 1957), *Sonzai* (Existence, 1961), and *Yami o Yami to shite* (Seeing the Dark as Dark, 1964).

Takenaka Iku was born on 1 April 1904 in the Hyōgo ward of Kōbe. His original name was Ishizaka, but he was adopted as an infant by his mother's sister's husband as his heir. His adoptive father was a manufacturer who made clay products for the spinning industry. He was attracted to poetry while at middle school by Kitahara Hakushū's work, and it was in the magazine *Shi to Ongaku* (Poetry and Music) which Hakushū edited that he appeared in 1923 as one of eleven rising young poets. In the same year he entered Kansei Gakuin to study English literature. Here with other former students of the Second Kōbe Middle School he established a Port Poets Club (Kaikō Shijin Kurabu), which published a magazine called *Rashin* (Compass Needle). Takenaka's first volume of poems, *Kibachi to Kafun* (Wasp and Pollen, 1926), was published by this Port Poets Club. His early works already showed a modern feeling, and while he was on a two-year tour of Europe (1928 –30), he was invited by Kondō Azuma (b. 1904) and Haruyama Yukio (b. 1902) to join *Shi to Shiron* (Poetry and Poetics). The poems which he sent to *Shi to Shiron* were collected in his *Zōge Kaigan* (Ivory Coast, 1931). In 1934 he became a member of the *Shiki* (Four Seasons) group. In the post-war period he has devoted himself especially to poetry for children; from 1948 he joined in editing a children's poetry magazine *Kirin* (Giraffe).

Tamura Ryūichi was born on 18 March 1923 in Ōtsuka, Tokyo. He graduated from the Third Tokyo Commercial School (1940) and afterwards from an Arts course in Meiji University (September 1943). At the end of 1943 he entered the Yokosuka Second Naval Barracks and served as an instructor with the Naval Flying Corps. When the war ended he worked for two or three years as head of the editorial department of the publishers Hayakawa Shobō. Later he became a lecturer at Tokyo Metropolitan University. His poetry career began before the war when, like his fellow-student at the Third Commercial School, Kitamura Tarō, he contributed to *Shin-ryōdo* (New Territory). With Kitamura he became a central member of the *Arechi* (Waste Land) group in the early post-war period. Later he joined Kusano Shinpei's *Rekitei*. Much of his earlier poetry was published in the *Arechi* anthologies. His first individual volume *Yonsen no Hi to Yoru* (Four Thousand Days and Nights) appeared in 1956 and was followed by *Kotoba no nai Sekai* (World Without Words, 1962), which shared the 1963 Takamura Kōtarō Prize, a *Poetical Works* in 1966, and *Midori no Shisō* (Green Thought, 1967). He has also published a volume of critical essays, *Wakai Arechi* (Young Waste Land, 1968), and many translations of English and American literature.

Tanaka Fuyuji was born on 13 October 1894 in Fukushima, where his father, a bank officer, was posted at the time. His father's next post (1897) took the family to Akita in northern Japan, and here he died in

1901. The family went to Tokyo, and Fuyuji had his middle school education there. He would have liked to study English at Waseda but instead entered his father's old bank (1913). His first post was at Imaichi in Western Japan; subsequently he served in Ōsaka (1920–22), Tokyo (1922–39), Nagano (1939–42), Suwa (1942–44), Kōriyama (1944–46), and Tokyo (1946–49). His poetry career began comparatively late, in 1921, when he first published in the important though short-lived magazine *Shisei* (The Saint of Poetry, 1921–23). Afterwards he contributed to *Panthéon* and *Orphéon*, and in 1929 published his first collection *Aoi Yomichi* (Travelling in the Blue Night). This has been followed by a dozen other volumes, including *Banshun no Hi ni* (On a Late Spring Day, 1961), which gained him the Takamura Kōtarō Prize for 1962. The chief characteristic of his poetry is a fresh and simple description of nature, yet one which shows the effect of the modernist tendency of the late 1920s.

Tanikawa Shuntarō was born on 15 December 1931 in Suginami, Tokyo, the eldest son of Tanikawa Tetsuzō (b. 1895), philosopher and writer on aesthetics. Growing up at the end of the war, he graduated with difficulty from the Toyotama High School. Yet, through the recommendation of Miyoshi Tatsuji, his "Nero" and five other poems were published in the important *Bungakkai* (Literary World) in 1950, and two years later his first collection *Nijū Oku Kōnen no Kodoku* (The Loneliness of Twenty Million Light Years) appeared. He became a member of the *Rekitei* group, but in the year of his second volume, *Rokujū-ni no Sonetto* (Sixty-two Sonnets, 1953), he joined *Kai* (Oar) and like other of its members began to write radio plays in verse (he afterwards moved also into television and films). He has produced four other volumes of poems, including *Tabi* (Journey, 1968) after his visit to Europe and America (1966–67). Tanikawa, by the vigour and range of his activity, has undoubtedly become the best-known poet of the post-war generation in Japan.

Tōge Sankichi (1917–10 March 1953). Born in Toyonaka, Ōsaka, he graduated from the Hiroshima Prefectural Commercial School. Afterwards he worked as a government clerk, in a publishing company, and for a newspaper. He was a victim of radiation sickness as a result of the Hiroshima atomic bomb. The poems of his *Gen-baku Shishū* (Atomic Bomb Anthology; first published 1951, reprinted with five additional poems, 1952) describe his personal experiences in a documentary style.

Tomioka Taeko was born on 28 July 1935 in Ōsaka, where she graduated in English Literature from the Ōsaka Women's College (1957). After graduation she taught for two years before moving to Tokyo, where she now lives. She began her poetry career like other young Ōsaka poets with the encouragement of Ono Tōzaburō. She gained early success with her first collection, *Henrei* (A Present in Return, 1957), which was awarded the eighth Mr H. Prize in 1958. The long poem *Monogatari no Akuru-hi* (The Day After the Story, 1960) won her a Murō Saisei Prize in 1961. She followed these with *Onna-tomodachi* (The Girl Friend, 1964), a *Poetical Works* (1967), and a volume of essays, *Nihon, Nihonjin* (Japan, Japanese, 1968).

Tsuchii (Doi) Bansui (23 October 1871–19 October 1952). Born Tsuchii Rinkichi, he changed the reading of his family name, because it was generally so misread, to Doi in 1934 (Bansui is a literary name). His early desire for advanced education was saved from frustration by the foundation of the English Academy in his native Sendai in 1887 and of the Second Higher School there in 1888. He graduated from the latter to the Department of English at Tokyo Imperial University in 1894. Here he became a member of the editorial staff of the newly founded literary magazine *Teikoku Bungaku*. His reputation as a writer of new poetry was quickly established (his first collection, *Tenchi Ujō*, The Sentient World, was published in 1899) and rivalled that of Shimazaki Tōson. His *"Kōjō no Tsuki"* (Moon over the Ruined Castle) was included in the Meiji *Middle School Song Collection* in 1901 and in consequence became the most widely known of his poems. He was appointed professor at his alma mater, the Second Higher School, in 1900 and here he remained until his retirement in 1934, apart from a four-year visit to Europe (1901–04) which produced his third volume of poems *Tōkai Yūshi Gin* (Songs of a Traveller from the Eastern Sea).

Unlike Tōson, he continued to publish volumes of poems throughout most of his long life; he also translated Homer from the Greek (*Iliad*, 1940, and *Odyssey*, 1943). But critics limit his significant activity to his early years, in which they contrast his Chinese-derived and so "masculine" style with the "femininity" of Tōson.

Yamamoto Tarō was born on 8 November 1925 in the Tokyo suburb of Ōmori. His father was the painter Yamamoto Kanae (1882 –1946); his mother was Kitahara Hakushū's younger sister. He graduated in German Literature from the University of Tokyo in 1949. In the same year he founded with others the magazine *Reido* (Zero, 1949–51). From 1950 he was a member of the *Rekitei* group. He edited the art journal *Atelier* for a number of years and later became a professor at Hōsei University. His first volume of poems, *Hokō-sha no Inori no Uta* (Songs of Prayer of a Pedestrian), appeared in 1954 and has been followed by some six others, including *Gorilla* (1960) which gained him a Takamura Kōtarō Prize. He has been the most prolific of the post-war poets.

Yamamura Bochō (10 January 1884–8 December 1924). Born the son of a countryman in Munadaka village in Gunma prefecture, Bochō looked back on a miserable boyhood. At the age of fifteen he was working as a temporary employee in the local primary school and two years later became an assistant teacher there. Acquaintance with Christian missionaries brought a change in his fortunes. In 1902 he was baptized and in the next year he was sent to the Holy Trinity Theological College in Tokyo, where he was attracted to the study of literature rather than to Greek and Hebrew. After serving in Manchuria during the Russo-Japanese War (1905–6), he returned to the Theological College. When he graduated in 1908 he was appointed to a church in Akita prefecture in north-western Japan. Afterwards he moved to Sendai (1909), Taira in Fukushima prefecture (1912), and Mito in Ibaraki prefecture (1918), living out a life of poverty and sickness. Bochō became a member of the Free Verse Society in 1910, and his poems produced an immediate shock in poetry circles. His works showed considerable shifts from the imagist technique of his first two collections,

Sannin no shojo (Three Virgins, 1913) and *Sei-sanryō-hari* (Holy Crystal, 1915), to the Dostoevsky-influenced humanism of *Kaze wa Kusaki ni Sasayaita* (The Wind Murmured among the Plants and Trees, 1918) and *Kozue no Su nite.* (In a Nest in the Tree-top, 1921) and to the quiet traditionalism of his last collection, *Kumo* (Clouds, 1924).

Yasumizu Toshikazu was born on 15 September 1931 in Kōbe and graduated in English and American Literature from Kōbe University. He followed an academic career and became professor at the Shōin Women's College in his home city. A post-war adherent of the *Rekitei* group, he published his first volume of poems, *Sonzai no tame no Uta* (Songs for Existence), in 1955 and five further volumes in the next eleven years.

Yosano Akiko, *née* Hō Shō (7 December 1878–29 May 1942). Born into an old-established merchant family with literary tastes in the city of Sakai, south of Ōsaka, as a child she showed a fondness for Japanese classics like *The Tale of Genji* (of which she was in later life to make several partial and finally a complete modern translation) and *The Pillow Book* of Sei Shōnagon. Her first published *tanka*-poem appeared in an anthology by a local Sakai society in 1896. Three years later she joined the Kansai Seinen Bungaku-kai (Kansai Young People's Literary Association) and published *shi*-poems in its magazine *Yoshiashi-gusa* (Indifferent Jottings). She was attracted to the romantic works of the *Bungakkai* (Literary World) writers and especially to Shimazaki Tōson's *Wakana-shū.* In 1900 she became a member of the New Poetry Society and a contributor (from the second issue) to its magazine *Myōjō* on the invitation of Yosano Tekkan (1873–1935), whom she married in the autumn of 1901 after he divorced his first wife. Her passionate love-affair with Yosano Tekkan produced her first and most famous *tanka* collection *Midare-gami* (Tangled Hair), which was edited by Tekkan and published under the imprimatur of the New Poetry Society in 1901. While Akiko, who thus established herself as the foremost romantic poet, continued to publish poetry, especially *tanka* (more than twenty collections) but also many *shi*, throughout her life, the days of the first series of *Myōjō* (1900–1908; Tekkan and Akiko revived it for six years from 1921) were her great period. After 1908 her activities became more diverse; she worked for women's education, she wrote many critical and other essays, she made translations of early Japanese classics. Yet her poetic style showed little change. A *shi*-poem which evoked strong criticism when it was published in *Myōjō* in 1904 amid the patriotic fervour of the Russo-Japanese War but which holds a place of esteem in Japanese anti-war literature is *Kimi Shinitamō koto nakare*.

Yoshihara Sachiko was born on 28 June 1932 in Tokyo and graduated from the University of Tokyo. Her first collection, *Yōnen Rentō* (Childhood Litany, 1964), gained her a Murō Saisei Prize in 1964, and ten years later she received a Takami Jun Prize. She has published three further collections.

Yoshino Hiroshi was born on 16 January 1926 in Sakata, Yamagata prefecture, on the north-western coast of the main island of Japan, where he graduated from the local commercial school. Immediately after the war he worked for a trade-union for three years but fell ill (1949) and underwent medical treatment in Tokyo. In hospital he met Tomioka Keiji and under his influence he began to write poetry. In 1953 he became a member of the *Kai* (Oar) group of young lyric poets. His first collection, *Shōsoku* (News), appeared in 1957, followed by *Maboroshi, Hōhō* (Illusions, Devices) in 1959. In 1962 he gave up being a "salary-man" and became a freelance copy-writer. His lyrics achieve a high degree of social consciousness and human sympathy expressed in a remarkably direct and simple language.

Yoshioka Minoru was born on 15 April 1919 in the Honjo ward of Tokyo. He entered a commercial high school but failed to complete the course. During the war he served in Manchuria. He began writing *tanka* and *haiku* while a schoolboy and published his first volume of *shi* in 1941. General recognition came to him in the 1950s when he published his second and third volumes, *Seibutsu* (Still Life, 1955) and *Sōryo* (Priests, 1958; this gained him the Mr H. Prize, 1959), and founded the magazine *Wani* (Crocodile; July 1959–September 1962) with Ōoka Makoto, Iwata Hiroshi, and others. After working for several publishers he became a director of the important Chikuma Shobō house.

Yoshiyuki Rie was born on 8 July 1939 in Tokyo and graduated in Japanese Literature from Waseda University in 1961. In 1963 she published her first collection, *Aoi Heya* (Blue Room). She followed this with *Yume no naka de* (In a Dream), which was awarded the Tamura Toshiko Prize in 1968. She published a *Poetical Works* in 1970. Besides poetry she has written fiction (her brother Yoshiyuki Junnosuke is a well-known novelist) and children's stories.

Zikkoku Osamu was born on 24 May 1915 in Kagawa prefecture, Shikoku. His poetry career dates from 1936, when he was a contributor to Kitagawa Fuyuhiko's *Pan* (Bread). From 1937 to 1946 he was a soldier and served in Manchuria and in Burma. After his demobilization he founded the magazine *Shi Kenkyū* (Poetry Research), which has continued up to the present, in Takamatsu. He has a strong interest in the democratization of Japan and in the reform of the writing system; he experiments with composing poems in *kana*. He is an admirer of William Carlos Williams.

Bibliography

Anthologies (including general anthologies of Modern Japanese literature that include poetry)

Keene, Donald, ed. *Modern Japanese Literature* New York: Grove Press, 1956.

Kōno Ichiro and Fukuda Rikutaro, eds. and trs. *An Anthology of Modern Japanese Poetry*, Tokyo: Kenkyusha, 1957.

Ninomiya Takamichi and Enright, D.J. *The Poetry of Living Japan*, London: John Murray, 1957.

Bownas, Geoffrey, and Thwaite, Anthony, trs. *The Penguin Book of Japanese Verse*, Harmondsworth, Mddx.: Penguin, 1964.

Fitzsimmons, Thomas, *Japanese Poetry Now*, London: Rapp and Whiting, 1972.

Guest, Harry, and Lynn and Kajima Shōzō, *Post-War Japanese Poetry*, Harmondsworth, Mddx.: Penguin, 1972.

Shiffert, Edith Marcombe, and Sawa Yūki, *Anthology of Modern Japanese Poetry*, Vermont and Tokyo: Tuttle, 1972.

Mishima Yukio and Bownas, Geoffrey, eds, *New Writing in Japan*, Harmondsworth, Mddx.: Penguin, 1972.

Wilson, Graeme, and Atsumi Ikuko, *Three Contemporary Japanese Poets*, London: London Magazine Editions, 1972 [Anzai Hitoshi, Shiraishi Kazuko and Tanikawa Shuntarō]

Sato Hiroaki, tr. *Ten Japanese Poets*, Hanover, New Hampshire: Granite Publications, 1973. [Takamura Kōtarō, Shiraishi Kazuko, Takiguchi Shūzō, Nishiwaki Junzaburō, Hagiwara Sakutarō, Ishihara Yoshirō, Tomioka Taeko, Yoshioka Minoru, Takahashi Mutsuo, and Miyazawa Kenji]

Kijima Hajime, ed. *The Poetry of Postwar Japan*. Iowa City: University of Iowa Press, 1975. Contains article *Hadaka no Gengo: The Naked Language of Postwar Japanese Poetry* by Roy Andrew Miller.

Individual Poets

Hagiwara Sakutarō *Face at the Bottom of the World and Other Poems*, translated by Graeme Wilson, Vermont and Tokyo: Tuttle, 1969.

Ishikawa Takuboku, *A Handful of Sand*, Translated by Sakanishi Shio, Boston: Marshall Jones, 1934.

————, *The Poetry of Ishikawa Takuboku*, translated by H.H. Honda, Tokyo: Hokuseido, 1959.

————, *A Sad Toy*, translated by Takamine Hiroshi, Tokyo: Tokyo News Service, 1962.

————, *Poems to Eat*, translated by Carl Sesar, Tokyo: Kodansha, 1966.

Kusano Shinpei, *Frogs and Others*, translated by Cid Corman and Kamaike Susumu, Tokyo: Mushinsha, 1969.

Miyazawa Kenji, *Spring and Asura*, translated by Sato Hiroaki, Chicago: Chicago Review Press, 1973.

Shimazaki Tōson, "Shimazaki Tōson's Four Collections of Poems", Translated by James R. Morita, *Monumenta Nipponica*, XXV, 3–4 (1970).

Takagi Kyōzō, *Selected Poems of Takagi Kyozo*, Introduced and Translated by James Kirkup and Nakano Michio, Cheadle, Cheshire: Carcanet Press, 1973.

Takahashi Mutsuo, *Poems of a Penisist*, translated by Sato Hiroaki, introduction by Burton Watson, Chicago Review Press, 1975.

Takahashi Shinkichi, *Afterimages*, translated by Lucien Stryk and Ikemoto Takashi, London: London Magazine Editions, 1971.

Yosano Akiko, *Tangled Hair*, translated by Sakanishi Shio, Boston: Marshall Jones, 1935.

————, *The Poetry of Yosano Akiko*, Translated by H.H. Honda, Tokyo: Hokuseido, 1957.

————, *Tangled Hair*, Translated by Sanford Goldstein and Shinoda Seishi, Lafayette, Indiana: Purdue University, 1971.

Yoshioka Minoru, *Lilac Garden*, translated by Sato Hiroaki, introduction by J. Thomas Rimer. Chicago Review Press, 1976.

Issues of Magazines etc. specially devoted to modern Japanese poetry

Chicago Review 25, no. 2 (1973) An Anthology of Modern Japanese Poets, translated by Sato Hiroaki.

The Literary Review (Fairleigh Dickenson University, Teaneck, New Jersey) 6, no. 1 (autumn 1962): Translations by Ueda Makoto.

New World Writing. Sixth Mentor Selection (New York: New American Library), 1954. Eight contemporary Japanese poets, selected by Kitasono Katsue.

Poetry (Chicago) 88 (May 1956): Contemporary Poetry in Japan, edited by Sato Satoru and Constance Urdang.

Poetry Australia (South Head Press, Sydney) 36–37 (double issue) December 1970. Translations and introduction by James Kirkup.

Westerly (University of Western Australia), Nedlands, W.A., September 1976. Translations by Graeme Wilson.

Studies

Keene, Donald, *Landscapes and Portraits* Tokyo and Palo Alto, Cal.: Kodansha, 1971: Contains "Modern Japanese Poetry", "Shiki and Takuboku", "The Sino-Japanese War of 1894–95 and Japanese Culture", and "Japanese Writers and The Greater East Asia War".

Sugiyama Yoko, "The *Wasteland* and Contemporary Japanese Poetry", *Comparative Literature* 13, no. 3 (summer 1961).

Bibliographies

Japan P.E.N. Club, comp. *Japanese Literature in European Languages*, Tokyo, 1961; supplement, 1964; further supplemented by *Japanese Literature Today*, no. 1 (March 1976).

Fujino Yukio, comp. *Modern Japanese Literature in Western Translations*, Tokyo: International House of Japan Library, 1972.

Rimmer, J. Thomas, and Morrell, Robert E. *Guide to Japanese Poetry*, Boston: G.K. Hall & Co., 1975.